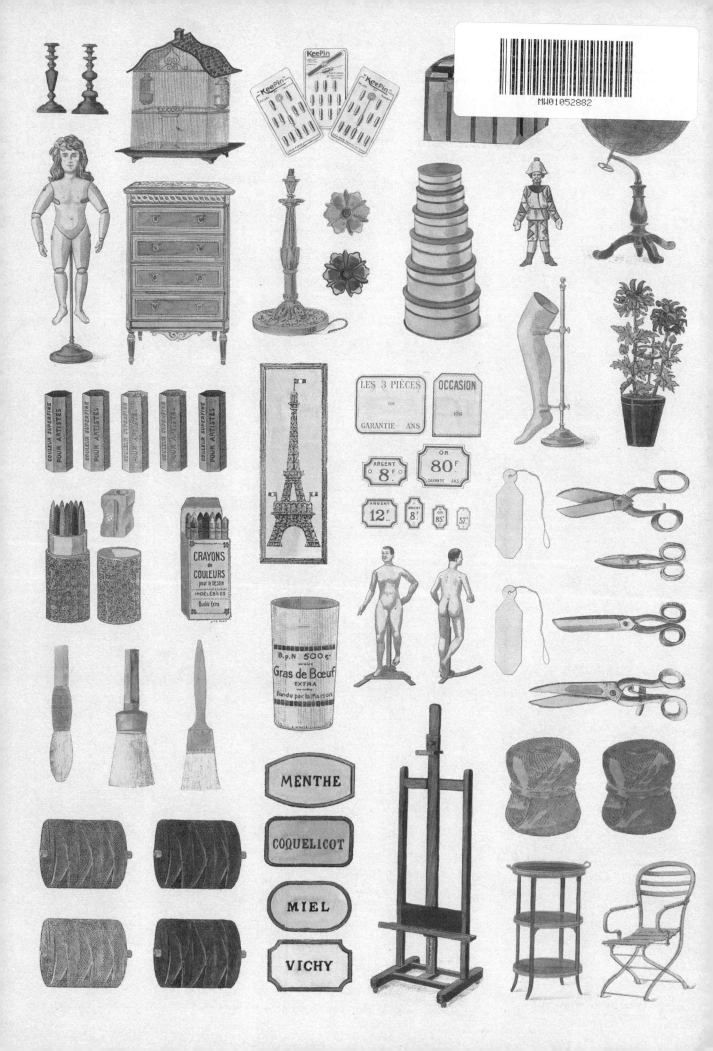

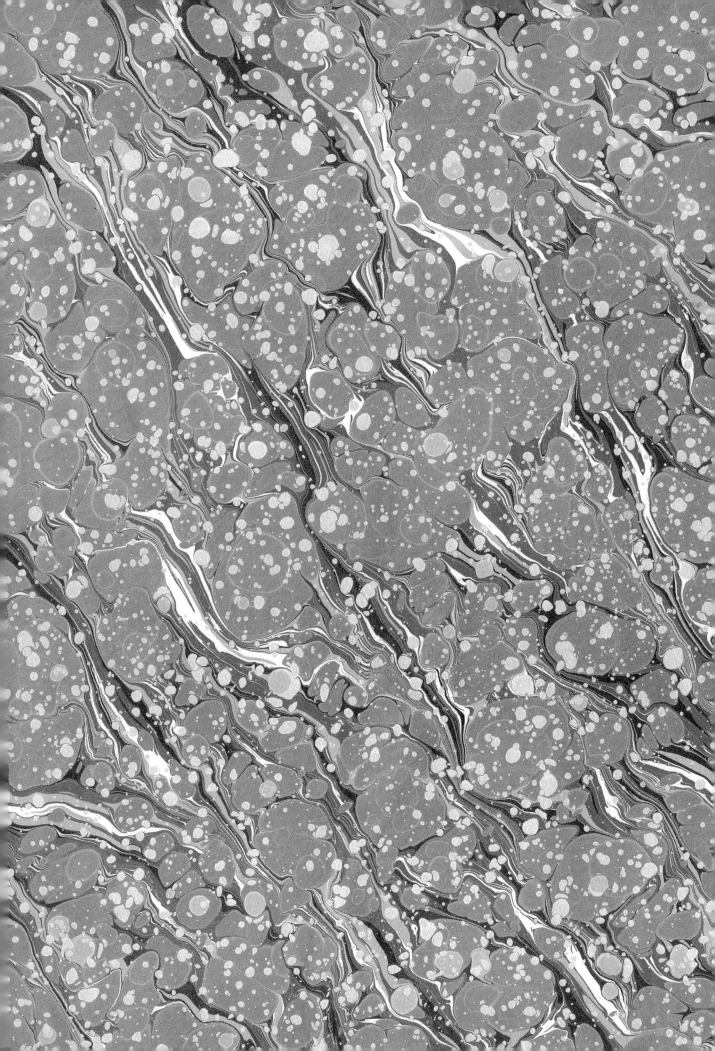

TIMELESS
PARIS

Editorial Director
Kate Mascaro

Editor
Helen Adedotun

Text
Laura Fronty

Translation from the French
Elizabeth Heard

Copyediting
Penelope Isaac

Design and Typesetting
Romain Chirat – Établissements Studio

Proofreading
Clodagh Kinsella

Production
Corinne Trovarelli and Élodie Conjat

Color Separation
Les Artisans du Regard

Printed in Portugal by
Printer Portuguesa

FRENCH EDITION

Editorial Director
Julie Rouart

Administration Manager
Delphine Montagne

Literary Director
Gaëlle Lassée
assisted by **Séléna Richez**

English-language edition
© Flammarion, S.A., Paris, 2021

Simultaneously published in French as
*Le Paris Merveilleux de Marin Montagut:
Échoppes et ateliers d'antan*
© Flammarion, S.A., Paris, 2021

© Adagp, Paris, 2021:
pp. 54, 58, 60: Maurice Utrillo; pp. 168–69:
Roger Bezombes, André Brasilier, Bernard
Buffet, Bernard Cathelin, Marc Chagall,
Constantin Terechkovitch; pp. 174–75:
Maurice Brianchon, Marc Chagall, Comité
Cocteau, Lennart Jirlow, Fernand Léger.

p. 175: © Françoise Gilot, *Tulips* and *Pineapple
and Watermelon*.

p. 197: © Serge Gainsbourg – With the kind
permission of Serge Gainsbourg's children:
self-portrait, 1957.

Baykul Baris Yilmaz created the marbled paper.

Ludovic Balay photographed the Musée de
Montmartre, Deyrolle, Ultramod, Féau & Cie,
Idem Paris, Académie de la Grande
Chaumière, and Produits d'Antan.

Pierre Musellec photographed La Maison
du Pastel, Passementerie Verrier, Musée de
Minéralogie, Librairie Jousseaume, Bouclerie
Poursin, À la Providence, Soubrier, Sennelier,
Herboristerie de la Place Clichy, Graineterie
du Marché, and Yveline Antiques.

Romain Ricard photographed the boutique
Marin Montagut.

editions.flammarion.com

22 23 24   4 3 2

ISBN: 978-2-08-020698-5

Legal Deposit: 10/2021

MARIN MONTAGUT

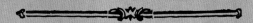

TIMELESS PARIS

ATELIERS • EMPORIUMS • SAVOIR FAIRE

PHOTOGRAPHY BY LUDOVIC BALAY,
PIERRE MUSELLEC, AND ROMAIN RICARD
—
ILLUSTRATIONS BY MARIN MONTAGUT

Flammarion

CONTENTS

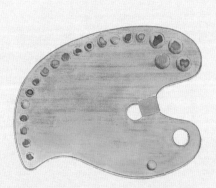
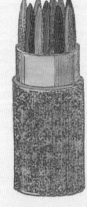

FÉAU & CIE   PAGE: 138

SOUBRIER   PAGE: 152

IDEM PARIS   PAGE: 164

SENNELIER   PAGE: 176

ACADÉMIE DE LA
GRANDE CHAUMIÈRE   PAGE: 188

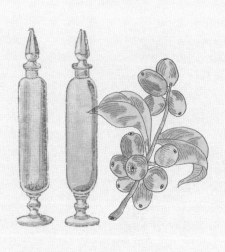

HERBORISTERIE
DE LA PLACE CLICHY   PAGE: 198

PRODUITS D'ANTAN   PAGE: 212

GRAINETERIE
DU MARCHÉ   PAGE: 220

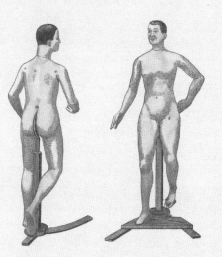

YVELINE ANTIQUES   PAGE: 228

MARIN MONTAGUT

48 RUE MADAME — PARIS 6ᴱ

I grew up in Toulouse, and, thanks to my parents, who were antique dealers, and my grandmother, who was an accomplished artist, I developed an appreciation for beautiful things at an early age. No detail escaped my notice and every object seemed to have its own tale to tell. But secretly I harbored the hope that, one day, I would live in Paris. I finally arrived in the City of Lights a few days after my nineteenth birthday, with little more than my paintbrushes and a box of watercolors.

Peering up at the blue and green enameled street signs, I learned the names by heart, so I could revisit them one day. I felt like I was immersed in a living postcard, from the metal chairs in the Luxembourg Gardens to the bridges over the Seine, and from the steeple of the Saint-Germain-des-Prés abbey to the Eiffel Tower. Instantly, I knew I could never live anywhere else—Paris was destined to be my forever home. I continued to explore the capital's byways over the years, determined to seek out the city behind the scenes, with all its secrets and surprises. Venturing across these thresholds, I found myself stepping into boutiques and workshops steeped in history and brimming with unexpected treasures. I encountered dedicated men and women who are the humble guardians of a priceless heritage of artisanal and ancestral expertise.

Inspired by these poignant discoveries, I decided to create a book to share and celebrate nineteen of these special places. Each of them is like a moment suspended in time, captured in photographs and illustrated by my watercolors and mood boards. I hope you'll steep yourself in their colors and ambiences, delight in fine craftsmanship, and lose yourself in a kaleidoscopic world of rare and extraordinary objects. All of these establishments are dedicated to preserving the soul of Paris. As you leaf through the book, you'll encounter hidden museums, traditional ateliers, and old-world emporiums.

Breathe in the irresistible fragrance of herbs and plants that
wafts from an herbalist's boutique near Place Clichy.
Follow in the footsteps of Colette and Cocteau, and let yourself
be enchanted by the array of rare, beautifully bound volumes
housed in a bookshop in the Galerie Vivienne. Time-travel to the
early twentieth century, to the Montparnasse of artists such as
Aragon, Man Ray, and Picasso: there, you'll visit a printer's
workshop and an art academy. Linger a while to enjoy the window
displays of an antique shop on Place Furstemberg, the most
charming square in Paris. Pause to view the legendary storefront
of a firm that, for almost two hundred years, has been devoted to
the sciences of taxidermy and entomology. Stroll along the banks
of the Seine and, not far from the École des Beaux-Arts, you'll
be delighted to enter—like Cézanne and Degas in their day—one
of the oldest artists' supply shops in Paris.

These timeless places and professions have been an inspiration
for my own creations. In the spirit of this Paris of yesteryear,
committed to traditional arts and craftmanship, I opened my
first store on Rue Madame, just steps away from the beautiful
Luxembourg Gardens that I hold so dear. It took me months
of searching to find the perfect spot: a former upholsterer's
workshop with an old-fashioned store window and façade.
I reconfigured the space to create three distinct rooms:
a curio shop, a boudoir, and a studio. With my passion for all
things from the past, I carefully restored the original parquet
floors and terra-cotta floor tiles, and salvaged pigeonhole
shelving from an old grocery store in the south of France to
display my treasures.

My favorite color is green, and I've used every shade, from
the palest to the deepest. I chose Parisian kiosk-green to frame
the glass partition in front of my studio. You can hear the creak
of ancient timber floorboards in my shop, and breathe in the
scent of old wood paneling. It's a voyage into a childhood
wonderland, recalling my youthful dreams of Paris.
The inscription on the façade of this modern-day store reads
"Purveyor of All Kinds of Objects." With my watercolors,
I conjure up items to brighten up my everyday life: stationery,
tableware, boxes, pillows, and silk scarves, each with a
different story to tell. My signature creations are entirely
handmade in my Montmartre studio, including the illusory "livres
à secrets" (hollow books), based on an eighteenth-century
tradition, and the "vitrines à merveilles" (wonder windows)
evoking imaginary escapades. I also bring back intriguing and
beautiful finds whenever I travel. My love of antique hunting,
which stems back to my childhood, has never left me. Each week,
I return laden with old globes, apothecary jars, insect display
cases, and other curiosities to delight my future visitors.

Nothing brings me more pleasure than seeing the treasures
displayed at 48 Rue Madame become your own cherished memories.
As for the destinations revealed in this book, I hope they will
inspire you to see Paris afresh and encourage you, in turn,
to venture through unfamiliar doorways.

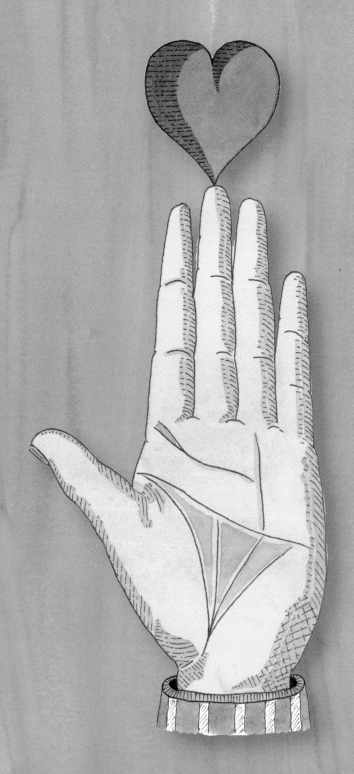

HANDCRAFTED

MARIN MONTAGUT

MARCHAND D'OBJETS
EN TOUS GENRES

SOUVENIRS DE PARIS
FAITS À LA MAIN

RÉF: 001

RÉF: 002

RÉF: 003

RÉF: 004

RÉF: 005

RÉF: 013

RÉF: 006

RÉF: 007

RÉF: 008

RÉF: 009

RÉF: 010

RÉF: 011

RÉF: 012

RÉF: 014

À QUELQUES PAS DU JARDIN DU LUXEMBOURG

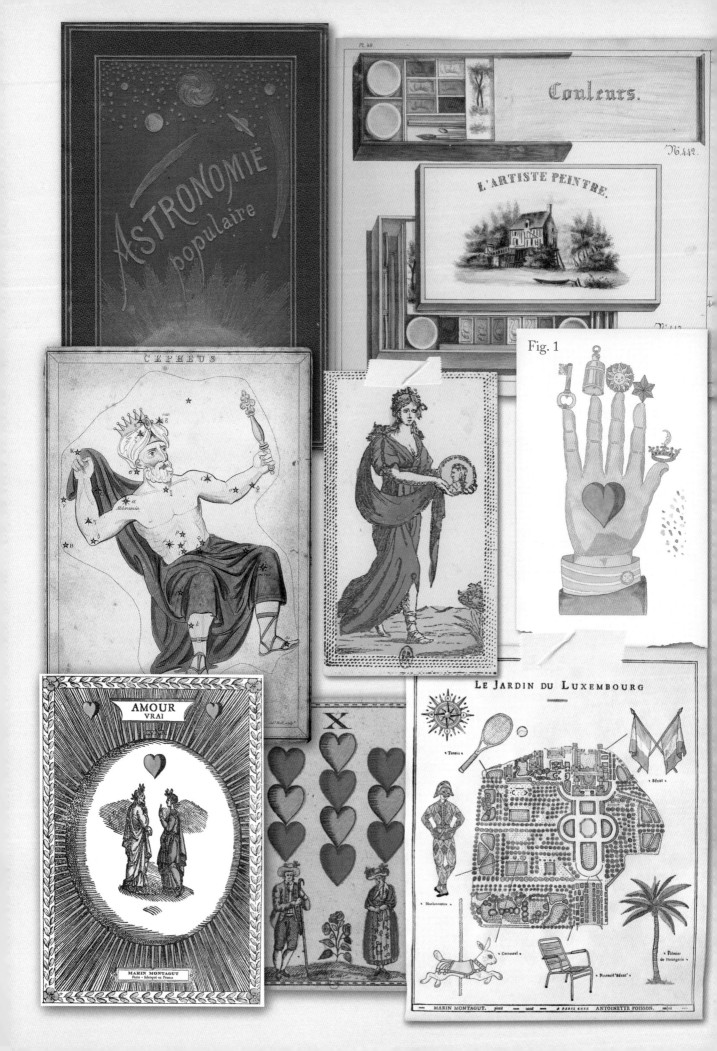

Fig. 2

Fig. 3

6ᵉ Arrᵗ
RUE
MADAME

AMOUR
MOU
A R
PARIS

MARQUIS DE ROCHEGUDE
PROMENADES
dans TOUTES les
Rues de Paris
PAR ARRONDISSEMENTS

6ᵉ ARRONDISSEMENT

NUIT.

JOUR.

MARIN MONTAGUT

SOUVENIRS
DE PARIS
FAITS
À LA MAIN

MARCHAND
D'OBJETS
EN TOUS
GENRES

À PARIS
48 RUE MADAME

LA MAISON DU PASTEL

20 RUE RAMBUTEAU — PARIS 3ᴱ

Open the door to this tiny boutique discreetly tucked away
in a cobblestone courtyard, and you'll be transported into the
history of a family that has been crafting pastels since 1870.
This was the year that Henri Roché—a pharmacist, biologist,
chemist, and art lover—decided to revive the business
of a legendary brand dating back to the eighteenth century.
The firm had been a purveyor to great artists including
Quentin de La Tour, Chardin, and later Degas. Roché introduced
new production processes based on scientific techniques that
enabled him to make richly colored pastel sticks, which were
prized by artists. His skills and secrets were passed down
through the generations, and a member of the Roché family
continues to manage the business today.
Isabelle Roché and her young American colleague, the artist
Margaret Zayer, personally welcome visitors into their small
shop. Nothing has changed here for one hundred fifty years.
The shelves are stacked with hundreds of boxes filled with
more than sixteen hundred subtly gradated shades. Everything
is hand-labeled. Twilight purple is stashed next to turtledove
gray, burnt umber, lichen and aphid greens: the names resonate
like tiny poems.
Isabelle and Margaret produce their pastels in a workshop
in the countryside. As with a culinary recipe, each stick
requires time, carefully measured ingredients, and scrupulous
attention to detail. Powdered pigments are weighed and blended
with water and a binder. This paste is processed through
a grinder and then combined with white in varying proportions
to create an almost infinite range of shades. The paste is
then pressed to extract excess moisture, hand-rolled, cut,
and dried. Each little stick bears evocative traces of the
hand that created it. Decades later, Isabelle still recognizes
the fingerprint of her cousins, or of Margaret, beside
the family seal: the hallmark "ROC" for Roché.

8341 Violet Intense
8361 Pourpre Impérial
8411 Violet Ara
8751 Caput Mortuum
8781 Violet Brûlé
4411 Ocre Citron

8591 Lie de Vin
8541 Violet Héliotrope
8631 Violet lointain

8721 Rose Passé
8741 Violet Van Dyck
8761 Violet de Mars

8821 Violet Prune
8841 Gris Tourterelle
8861 Violet Crépuscule

8961 Gris Carmin clair
9141 Noir Intense   8981 Gris Souris
9161 Noir Velours

9244 Blanc de Lys
9181 Noir Extra   9239 Blanc Intense
9121 Noir bleu

8881 Violet Horizon
8921 Teinte neutre
8941 Gris de Laque

L 7331 BLEU OUTREMER

In a pretty cardboard container embellished with art deco
motifs, these Roché pastels represent over one hundred fifty
years of artistic expertise.

orangé clair

orangé brillant

orangé foncé

5271 Vert au Violet

5291 Vert orangé

5261 Vert au Rouge

e Pise

l'Avignon

clair

5391 Vert Algue

5411 Vert doré

5431 Vert Pomme

rangé

dmium

une

LA MAISON DU PASTEL

PARIS

H. ROCHE

PASTELS-ROCHÉ

BOITES COMPOSEES
ET DETAIL

EN VENTE ICI

ne d'Or

ne Citron

e Canari

PASTELS
TENDRES ET DEMI-DURS
A LA GERBE
S. MACLE
PARIS

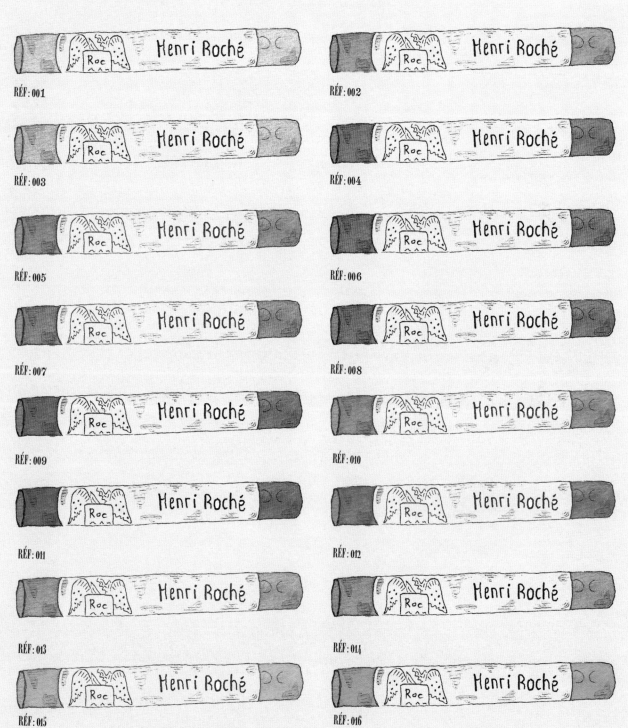

RÉF: 001

RÉF: 002

RÉF: 003

RÉF: 004

RÉF: 005

RÉF: 006

RÉF: 007

RÉF: 008

RÉF: 009

RÉF: 010

RÉF: 011

RÉF: 012

RÉF: 013

RÉF: 014

RÉF: 015

RÉF: 016

N.B — Les teintes marquées d'une Astérisque se font seules en crayons demi-durs.

Fig. 1

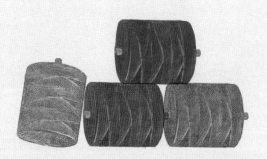

PASSEMENTERIE VERRIER

10 RUE ORFILA — PARIS 20ᴱ

The twentieth arrondissement of Paris was once home to numerous passementerie workshops, creating braid and other ornamental trimmings. Maison Verrier has been located on Rue Orfila, a stone's throw from the Père-Lachaise cemetery, since 1901. Verrier is a survivor from a lost era–a golden age when furnishings and apparel were richly embellished with decorative edging fashioned from silk, cotton, wool, and metal threads. The art of passementerie lives on here today.
Verrier's ancestral expertise and age-old techniques have survived the passage of time. More than three hundred styles of braid are produced in this spacious workshop. Its twenty wooden Jacquard looms, named after their inventor, date from the nineteenth century. The traditional system of perforated cards continues to function as efficiently as ever, as threads are interwoven with unerring precision.
Aside from the braid, everything is made by hand. Skillful craftswomen known as *établisseuses* (assemblers) and *enjoliveuses* (embellishers) have a golden touch and unparalleled dexterity, dipping into boxes of colored threads to create hundreds of tiebacks, cords, rosettes, and elaborate pom-poms sumptuously trimmed with smooth or twisted fringes, to adorn a headboard, hold back a drapery, or decorate a pillow. Anne Anquetin decided to acquire this extraordinary business in 2018. She prides herself on making exact reproductions of traditional designs on demand, but she is also intent on devising the passementerie creations of tomorrow. Contemporary decorators flock here for modern designs, featuring wood, leather, glass, and feathers instead of traditional materials.

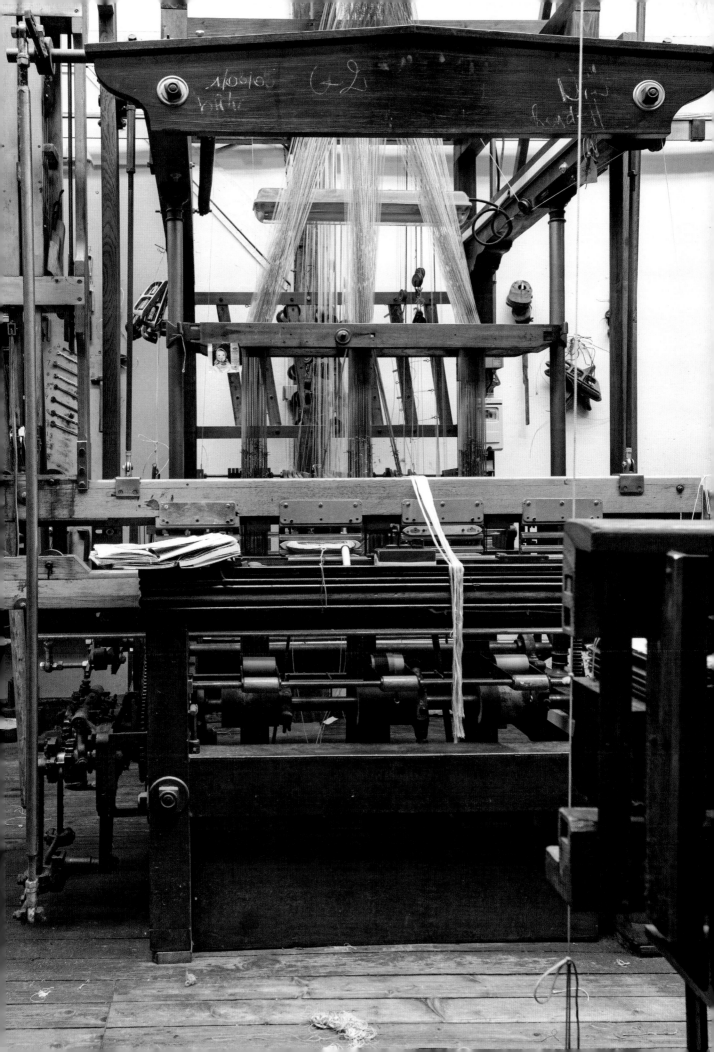

FABRIQUE DE PASSEMENTERIE D'AMEUBLEMENT

G. L. VERRIER FRERES & Cie

Société à Responsabilité Limitée au Capital de 10.000 Frs

10, Rue Orfila - PARIS-XXe

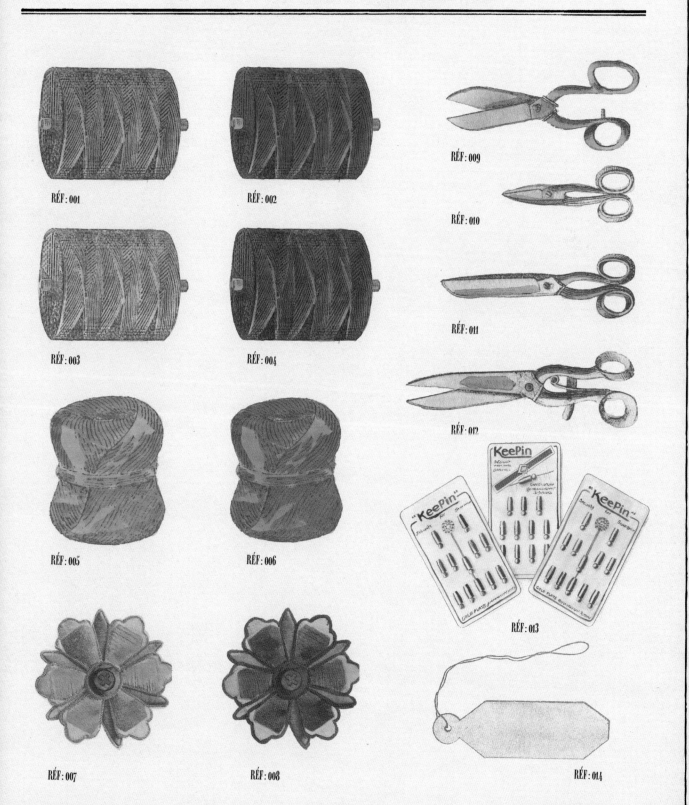

RÉF: 001

RÉF: 002

RÉF: 009

RÉF: 010

RÉF: 003

RÉF: 004

RÉF: 011

RÉF: 012

RÉF: 005

RÉF: 006

RÉF: 013

RÉF: 007

RÉF: 008

RÉF: 014

Galon Nº **242**

16 lisières. 28 fonds. 15 gantes

8 lisières. 1 gauze. 2 fonds. etc. 2 fonds. 1 gauze
8 lisières

Galon Nº **243**

2 fonds de 24 fls. 1 luisant de 24 fls par 2 coups
1 luisant de 14 fls (milieu) 6 gauzes

6 lis. 1 gauze. 2 fonds. 1 gauze. 2 fonds. 1 gauze. 14 fonds
12 luisants. 2 coups. 14 luisants

Galon Nº **244**   double figures

2 fonds de 22 fls. 1 large de 16 fls.
2 figures de 32 fls.

6 lisières. 8 larges. 32 figures double chaîne
la diagonale commence

Galon Nº **245**   si les luisants sont en poils
ouvrés à fl

12 lisières. 2 figures de 32 fls.

Embrasses **53**   Nº **246**

Existe en 1100

Embrasses **83**   Nº **247**

Passementerie.

Fig. 1

Tapisserie de Haute-Lisse des Gobelins.
Construction des Lices.

1793   1794

1795   1796

1797   1798

1799   1800

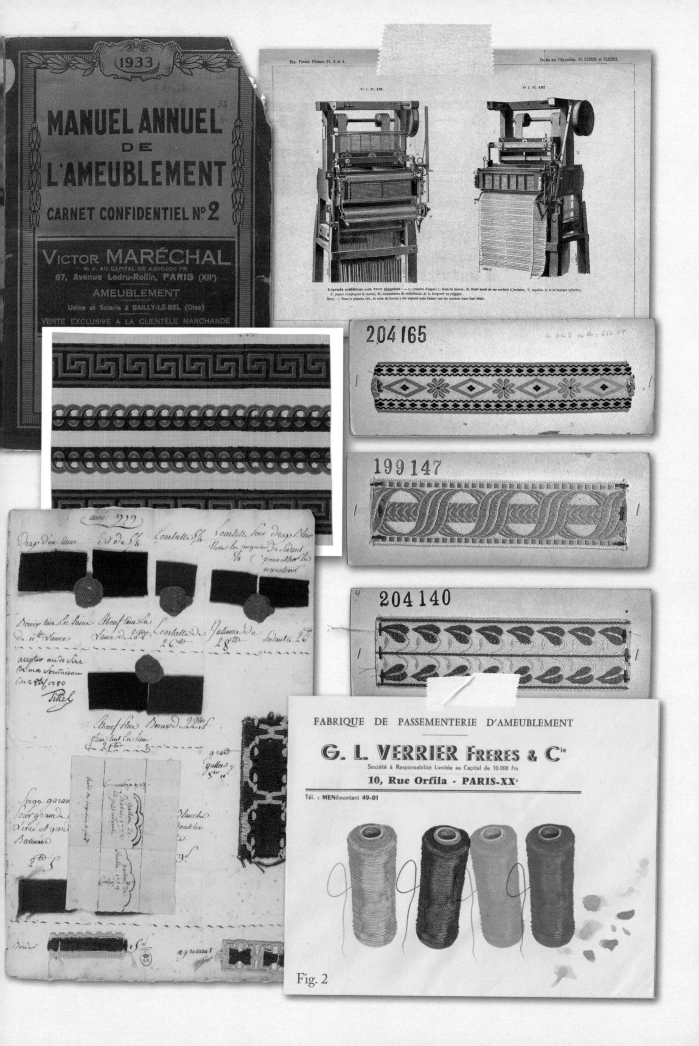

MUSÉE DE MONTMARTRE

12 RUE CORTOT — PARIS 18ᴱ

Tucked away at the end of an old cobbled street,
the Musée de Montmartre recalls a time when the rustic
butte was filled with windmills, willow trees, fields, and
vineyards. Artists of the late nineteenth and early twentieth
centuries relished the hillside's bucolic atmosphere. Renoir
was among the earliest painters to move here. Later, between
1912 and 1926, Suzanne Valadon, her son Maurice Utrillo,
and her husband André Utter lived in one of the studios.
Beautiful and heedless of social conventions, Suzanne Valadon
charted her own course as a painter. Starting out as a circus
acrobat, and later becoming an artist's model, she learned
painterly techniques by observing the artists she posed
for, including Puvis de Chavannes, Toulouse-Lautrec, and
Renoir. Encouraged by Cézanne and Degas, she began to paint
independently and became known for her landscapes,
still lifes, flower bouquets, and female nudes.
A flight of stairs leads to her modest apartment, with its
floral wallpaper, and to her studio, which has been faithfully
reconstructed by the designer and scenographer Hubert Le Gall,
based on the artist's canvases and contemporary photographic
documentation. The floorboards creak beneath your feet, and
the air is suffused with the distinctive aroma of turpentine.
It's easy to imagine Valadon painting in the company of Utter
and Utrillo. The illusion is sustained by the easels and
frames stacked up in a mezzanine above. A little Godin stove
once provided a modicum of warmth; the studio's vast windows
overlook a breathtaking panorama, but the winters must have
been bitterly cold.
On the ground floor, the museum displays temporary exhibitions
and houses the Café Renoir. The building's terraced gardens
offer views over Paris and the vineyards of Montmartre.
In springtime and summer, water lilies bloom in the little pond
and, under the arbor, the fragrance of roses perfumes the air.

Suzanne Valadon, who painted in an era when few women
were professional artists, was known for her portraits,
landscapes, and floral pieces, like this colorful
mixed bouquet in a clear vase.

EASELS

Until the nineteenth century, artists recreated
landscapes and natural scenes in their studios.
Portable folding easels, introduced around 1857,
allowed them to work outside and paint *en plein air*—
a practice embraced by the impressionists.

Set designer Hubert Le Gall deployed found objects to recreate
the singular atmosphere of an early twentieth-century Parisian studio.
The view of old Montmartre was painted by Maurice Utrillo.

MATÉRIEL POUR ARTISTES

COULEURS EXTRA-FINES EN TUBES BROYÉES À L'HUILE

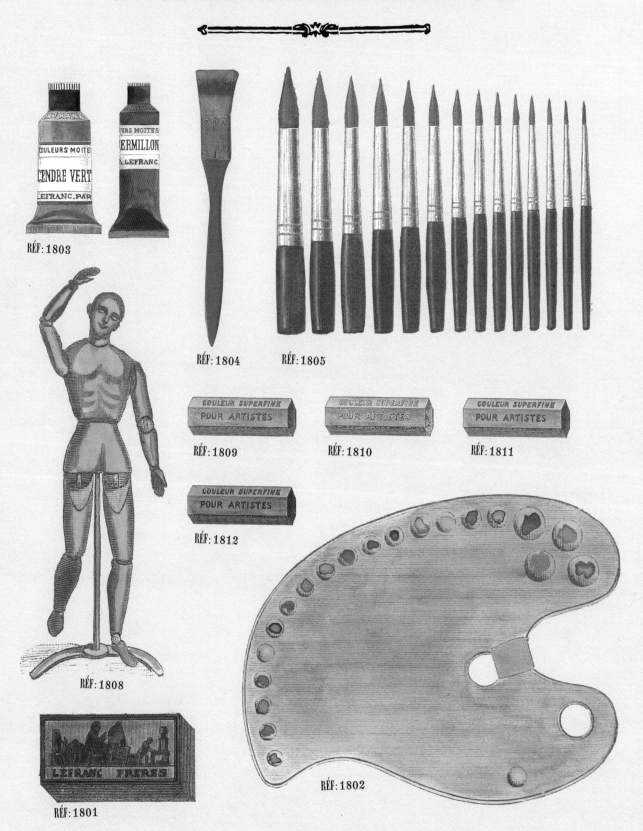

RÉF: 1803

RÉF: 1804

RÉF: 1805

RÉF: 1809

RÉF: 1810

RÉF: 1811

RÉF: 1812

RÉF: 1808

RÉF: 1802

RÉF: 1801

POUR LES DIMENSIONS ET LES QUALITÉS DIVERSES DES ARTICLES FIGURANT À CE CATALOGUE CONSULTER LE TARIF CI-JOINT.

Fig. 1

GEORGES MONTORGUEIL

La Vie
à Montmartre

ILLUSTRATIONS DE

PIERRE VIDAL

MUSÉE DE MINÉRALOGIE

60 BOULEVARD SAINT-MICHEL — PARIS 6ᴱ

This is a timeless place–a well-kept secret known only
to a few initiates. Established in 1794, the Musée de
Minéralogie was originally an educational establishment,
where students and researchers could learn about the world
of minerals. Housed in the stately Hôtel de Vendôme, this
impressive mineral collection is displayed in a 260-foot-long
(80-meter) gallery with windows overlooking the Luxembourg Gardens.
The glass cabinets and display cases exhibit several thousand
specimens, including wondrous objects from the innermost
depths of the earth, or even from the cosmos–the collection
includes meteorites. There are also precious gems from
the crown jewels of France: emeralds, topazes,
and amethysts. Other rocks are more unassuming
in appearance, but nevertheless stimulate
the imagination. The eye might conjure up a prehistoric
sculpture, an abstract painting, a star, or perhaps a tree.
This museum embraces art and science, but it also
encourages technological innovation in the service of
industry. The drawers, which are open to researchers, contain
almost one hundred thousand specimens. Violaine Sautter, a
specialist in planetary geology at France's Centre National
de la Recherche Scientifique (CNRS), came here to find samples
that served to design the laser device used on NASA's 2020
Mars mission. As visitors explore the museum's collections,
they receive a lesson in serenity and permanence:
a reminder that, long before there was air and
water, stones were at the origin of the world.

SALLE J

Confiscations

révo

The entrance hall of the Musée de Minéralogie displays
some of the most remarkable mineral specimens in this unique
collection—a strange and fascinating array of wonders.

LE MONT-BLANC VU DU GRAMONT

MUSÉE DE MINÉRALOGIE

CURIOSITÉS MINÉRALES

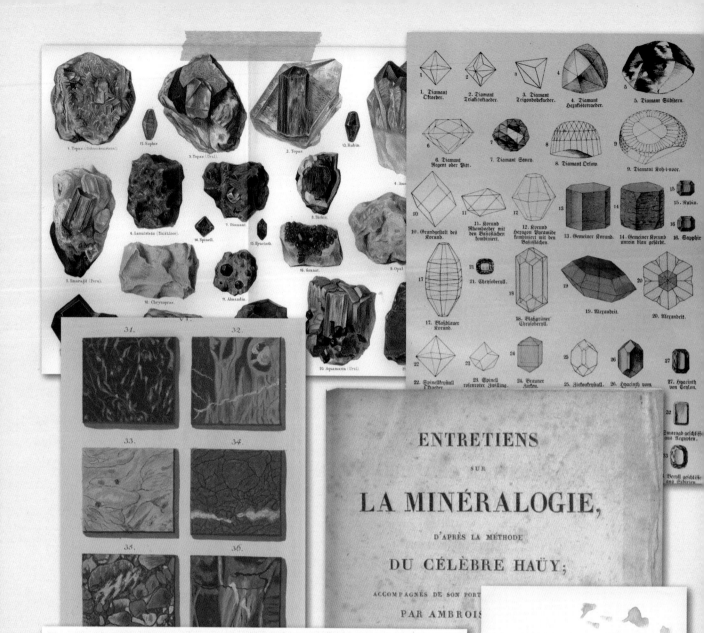

Fig. 1

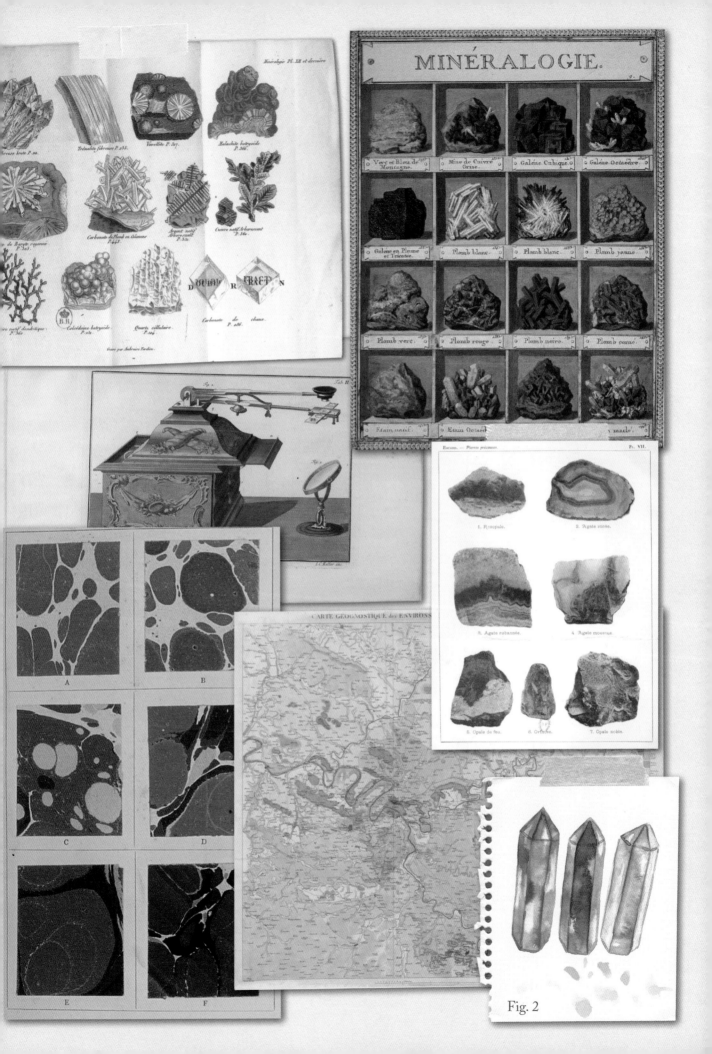

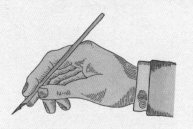

LIBRAIRIE JOUSSEAUME

45–47 GALERIE VIVIENNE — PARIS 2ᴱ

When Galerie Vivienne was inaugurated in 1826, it was considered the capital's loveliest covered passageway, admired for its neoclassical decor, antiquity-inspired mosaic floor, cupola, and glass roof, which casts radiant natural light over shoppers and passersby.
The Librairie Petit-Siroux, as the bookstore was called when it first opened, was an original tenant of the passageway, and that name still appears above the store's window.
It was a neighborhood institution, with two shops facing each other, at the foot of a few steps. François Jousseaume's great-grandfather acquired the business in 1890. A true bibliophile who loves his work, François cherishes childhood memories of the store. It is a place steeped in history, situated close to key sites such as the Bibliothèque Nationale de France, the Palais-Royal, and the Grands Boulevards.
"It was one of the Right Bank's cultural landmarks," he explains. "As in all the covered passages back then, there were publishers, engravers, printers, and bookshops, like my own family's. Colette and Cocteau would come here to browse together like neighbors."
There are thousands of used books—both antique and more recent—in this generalists' treasure trove. Visitors have access to a wide-ranging choice of subjects, including natural history, sociology, and art history, as well as fiction and poetry. Intrigued by Asian culture, François Jousseaume particularly enjoys recommending Lafcadio Hearn's work to his clients. Hearn was a Greco-Irish author who led a storybook life and collected traditional Japanese tales. And those tempted by adventure stories should consider books by sailor and writer Joseph Conrad, famed for *Lord Jim*, among other works. The curious visitor will wander to and fro between the two bookshops, and climb the spiral staircase that leads to the mezzanine, where an impressive collection of paperbacks includes the first work in Hachette's collection "Le Livre de Poche": *Kœnigsmark*, which was published in 1953, with its original cover.

BOOKS

"If you are lucky enough to have lived
in Paris as a young man, then wherever you go
for the rest of your life, it stays with you,
for Paris is a moveable feast."
Ernest Hemingway

ARTICLES POUR LIBRAIRIE
JOUSSEAUME

QUALITE EXTRA

			la douz.				la douz.
Nᵒˢ 000 diam.	16 ᵐ/ᵐ.	**5 50**	Nᵒˢ 2 diam.	24 ᵐ/ᵐ..	**10 50**
00	—	18	. **6** »	3	—	26	... **13** »
0	—	20	. **8** »	4	—	28	... **15** »
1	—	22	. **9 50**	5	—	30	... **19** »

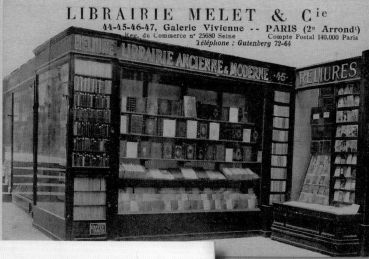

DU MONDE ENTIER

ERNEST HEMINGWAY

Paris
est une fête

TRADUIT DE L'ANGLAIS
PAR MARC SAPORTA

Fig. 1

LAFCADIO HEARN

Le Japon

TRADUIT DE L'ANGLAIS PAR
MARC LOGÉ

ŒUVRES DE VICTOR HUGO — NOTRE-DAME DE PARIS 1

ŒUVRES DE VICTOR HUGO — NOTRE-DAME DE PARIS II

CARTE D'EXPOSANT.
Signature du titulaire :

Fig. 2

BOUCLERIE POURSIN

35 RUE DES VINAIGRIERS — PARIS 10^E

Bouclerie Poursin is a "living treasure"
of traditional artisanship. Founded in 1830, it has been
in its current premises on Rue des Vinaigriers since
1890—the oldest workshop of its kind in Paris.
Originally, the firm produced saddlery accessories for use
by the cavalry. Several vitrines display memorabilia from
the time when Poursin made equipment for the Royal,
Imperial, and later Republican Guards. When cars superseded
horses, the firm shifted its focus to leather goods. While
it still retains the distinction of equipping the Republican
Guard, the Cadre Noir de Saumur riding academy, stud farms,
and various royal courts, it has also supplied great design
houses for decades, including Chanel, Hermès, and Louis Vuitton.
True luxury is often hidden in minute details, like Poursin's
signature buckle with its beveled brass prong. "Our version
caresses the leather without scratching it," explains Karl Lemaire.
In 2016, he became proprietor of the company, which was
in danger of folding. Lemaire, who is devoted to fine
workmanship and French tradition, had previously rescued
another legendary firm, Daudé, which invented a special
metal grommet and rivet in 1928.
In the workshop, he has preserved the powerful metal-stamping
machines as well as the original cast-iron molds. Mounted
on the walls, they present an impressive array. Catalogs
dating from the late nineteenth century, which include over
sixty thousand pieces, demonstrate the firm's time-honored
expertise. "At Poursin, past and present are one," Karl
Lemaire confirms. Everything is made the old-fashioned way,
from cutting and bending the brass wire on the old machines
to the subsequent soldering and polishing that are carried out
by hand. In the drawers of a chest dating from 1830, models
from long ago can be found. It is like diving into the heart
of Parisian history.

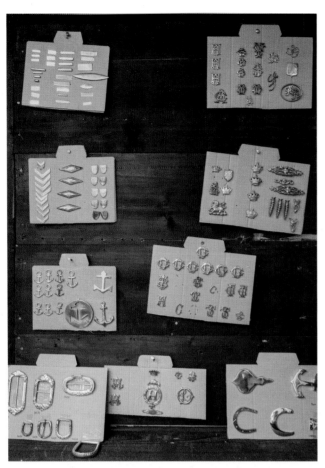

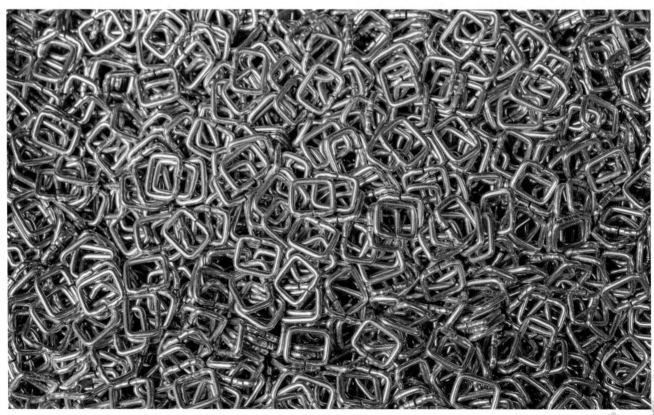

The workshop's machines produce three hundred thousand
pieces daily. Piled high in a crate, these brass buckle
frames await assembly.

TOUTE LA BOUCLERIE et la CUIVRERIE

S. POURSIN

35, Rue des Vinaigriers — PARIS (Xe) — Nord: 17-07

RÉF: 001

RÉF: 002

RÉF: 003

RÉF: 005

RÉF: 006

RÉF: 004

RÉF: 007

RÉF: 008

*Plus de cent années
de Technique ...
et de belle fabrication*

Alphonse

MANUFACTURE DE BOUCLERIES
POUR HARNACHEMENTS

CUIVRERIE, NICKEL & PLAQUÉ ARGENT
POUR
SELLERIE

GARNITURES POUR HARNAIS
de tous genres et de tous modèles

CHIFFRES & ORNEMENTS
COCARDES, CONTOURS, ETC.

E. DAVID & POURSIN, 35, Rue des Vinaigriers, PARIS

TÉLÉPHONE 359-47

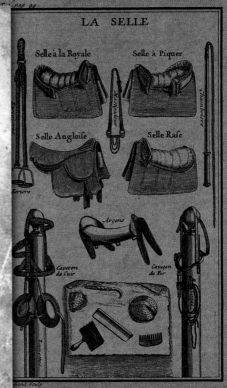

LA SELLE

Selle à la Royale   Selle à Piquer

Selle Angloise   Selle Rase

Arçons

Caveçon
de Cuir   Caveçon
                      de Fer

ouvrage de phidias

THE
RSE OWNER'S
FRIEND
BY
L. R. HERRICK,
NEW YORK.

PAROLE.
THE GREAT AMERICAN RUNNING HORSE

All the Remedies described in this book are for sale by

J. C. KUYKENDAL,
APOTHECARY,
YORKVILLE, S. C.

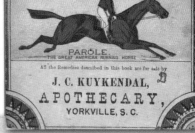

639/25   273/25   503/25

631/25   249/20   618

et trois boucles
à gainer

KRONEN. I.

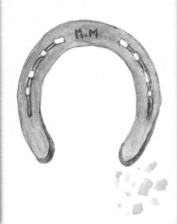

Fig. 1

M.M

Edward the Confessor.   Edward the Confessor.

Henry II.   John.   Henry III.

Edward II.   Richard II.   Henry IV.

Henry V.   Henry VII.   Charles II.

CROWNS OF THE KINGS OF ENGLAND.

"Long to rein over us!"

Tho' he's kicking o'er the trace,
Smites the wheeler in the face,
   Short his pranks will be:
For such hands the reins as hold –
Little, pretty, firm and bold –
   Rule even you and me!

Side-ways
Hind-ways.
graceful form.

Fig. 2

PLANCHE XV

Fig. 2

RACES _ 1. CHEVAL ARABE _ 2. CHEVAL ANGLO-NORMAND.
Publié par J.B. Baillière & fils à Paris

Imp. Lemercier & Cie Paris

DEYROLLE

46 RUE DU BAC — PARIS 7ᴱ

Deyrolle is a cabinet of curiosities like no other in the
world. It is surely the only place in Paris where one can
see a donkey paying court to a lioness, while an albino
peacock poses a few feet away from a polar bear. Beneath
glass bell jars, magnificent Brazilian blue butterflies take
flight, while lobsters and spider crabs suggest the forms of
contemporary sculptures. Meticulously arranged in their cases,
scarabs shimmering with hues of gold, bronze, and emerald are
displayed like natural precious gems.

The firm, founded in 1831, originally specialized in taxidermy
and selling supplies for natural history collections.

In 1888, the shop moved to an old town house on Rue du Bac.
In addition to its collections of insects and stuffed animals,
the company also had an educational mission, producing and
selling wall prints and specialized works on flora and fauna.

In 2001, Louis Albert de Broglie bought the internationally
renowned firm, which attracted scientists, students of
entomology, and curious visitors with the beauty and ambience
of the collections housed amid magnificent eighteenth-century
paneling. Since 2007, Deyrolle pour l'Avenir (Deyrolle for the
Future), instigated by Louis Albert de Broglie,
has perpetuated the firm's instructional calling, reinventing
it with custom-designed prints dedicated to the preservation
of our planet.

Tragically, very early one morning in 2008, a fire broke
out in the store. The cabinet of entomology and 90 percent
of the collection were reduced to ashes. Great design houses
and artists rallied to save this legendary site, and
a benefit auction was organized. The funds raised were used
to restore the devastated premises, reconstitute a collection,
and reproduce the old wall prints. Today, as in the past,
new generations continue to fall under the spell of this
enchanting place.

A magical place, where visitors encounter creatures
and natural objects from all over the world,
in a wonderland of shapes and colors.

TAXIDERMY

The taxidermist's art entails creating
the illusion of life, as skilled hands
seemingly revive animal bodies. None of
Deyrolle's creatures was deliberately killed;
they all died of natural causes.

Eterusia
repleta
(Thailande)
ZYG10208   25€
DEYROLLE - 46, Rue du Bac, PARIS VII

Delias timorensis
moaensis
(Mex-Indonésie)
PIE10299   30€
DEYROLLE - 46, Rue du Bac, PARIS VII

Phoebis philea
(Pérou)
PIE10102   35€
DEYROLLE - 46, Rue du Bac, PARIS VII

Papilio
oribazus
(Madagascar)
PAP10303   15€
DEYROLLE - 46, Rue du Bac, PARIS VII

Chetone sp.
(Pérou)
ERE10102   35€
DEYROLLE - 46, Rue du Bac, PARIS VII

Hebomoia leucippe
(Indonésie)
PIE10209   35€
DEYROLLE - 46, Rue du Bac, PARIS VII

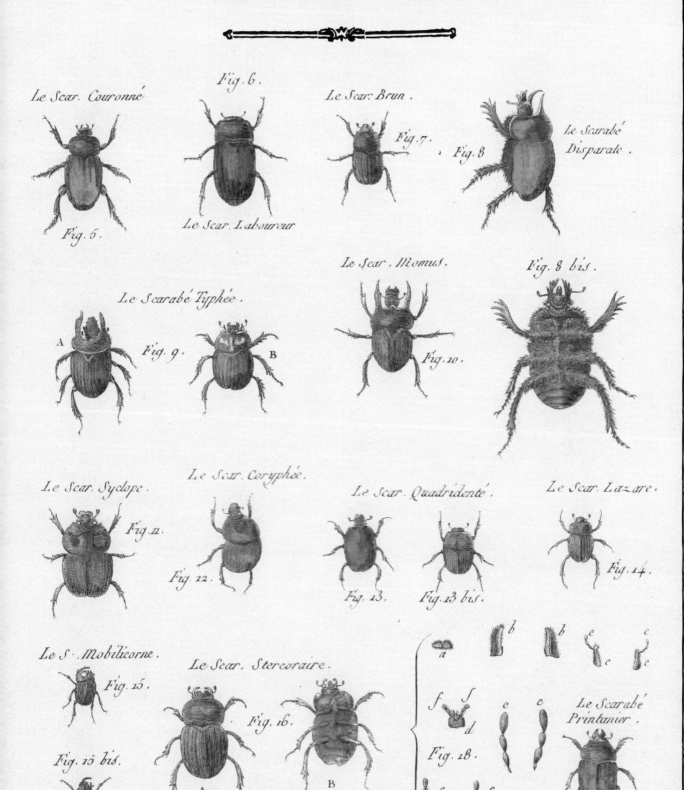

Le Scar. Couronné

Fig. 6.

Le Scar. Brun.

Fig. 7.

Fig. 8

Le Scarabé Disparate.

Fig. 5.

Le Scar. Laboureur

Le Scarabé Typhée.

Le Scar. Momus.

Fig. 8 bis.

A

Fig. 9.

B

Fig. 10.

Le Scar. Syclope.

Le Scar. Coryphée.

Le Scar. Quadridenté.

Le Scar. Lazare.

Fig. 11.

Fig. 12.

Fig. 13.

Fig. 13 bis.

Fig. 14.

Le S. Mobilicorne.

Le Scar. Stercoraire.

Fig. 15.

Fig. 16.

Le Scarabé Printanier.

Fig. 15 bis.

A

B

Fig. 18.

Fig. 17.

NAIRE

RELLES,

ACQUISITION
9280406.

…ENS ÊTRES DE LA NATURE
…D'APRÈS L'ÉTAT ACTUEL D…
…IVEMENT À L'UTILITÉ QU'E…
…, L'AGRICULTURE, LE COMMERC…

SUIVIE DE LA BIOGRAPHIE DES PLUS CÉLÈBRES
…TES.

…commerçans
…i ont intérêt
…res génériqu…
…eurs usages.

…s principales

…liteur.
…° 8.

Pl.120

Fig. 2
Le Figuier bleu

Fig. 1.ere
La Fauvette verte

Fig. 3
Le Figuier à tête cendrée

Fig. 4
Le Figuier tacheté de jaune

Histoire Naturelle, Ornithologie.

Psittacus.
Perroquet vert.

HISTOIRE NATURELLE
DE LA
FRANCE
7e PARTIE
MOLLUSQUES
(BIVALVES)
TUNICIERS, BRYOZOAIRES
AVEC 18 PLANCHES
PAR
ALBERT GRANGER
MEMBRE DE LA SOCIÉTÉ LINNÉENNE DE BORDEAUX

Fig. 1

23   ARTICULÉS

177	178	179	180
CÉRAMBIX	COCCINELLE	TERMITE	PUCE
181	182	183	184
COURTILIÈRE	CURUS	CIGALE	CRABE

G. EISENMENGER ET H. COUPIN

LES
SCIENCES NATURELLES
DES COURS COMPLÉMENTAIRES
ET DE L'ENSEIGNEMENT PRIMAIRE SUPÉRIEUR
BREVET ÉLÉMENTAIRE
(LES TROIS ANNÉES RÉUNIES)

PARIS

Pl. 57.

Fig. 2. L'Élan

Fig. 1ʳᵉ Le Pygargue

Fig. 4. La Biche

Fig. 3. Le Cerf

Histoire Naturelle, Quadrupèdes.

Fig. 2

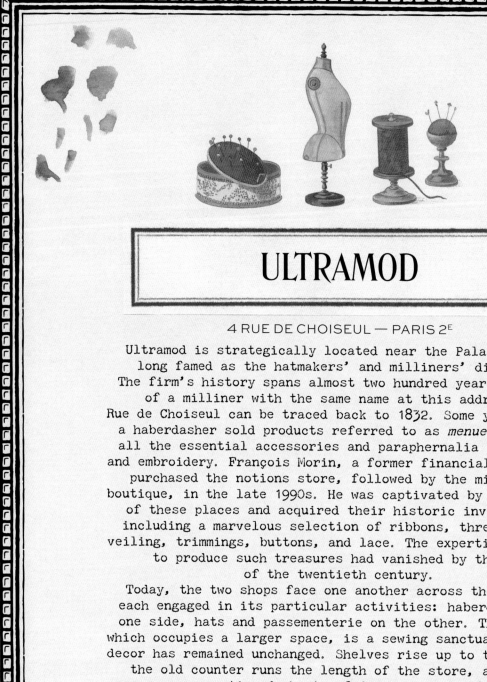

ULTRAMOD

4 RUE DE CHOISEUL — PARIS 2ᴱ

Ultramod is strategically located near the Palais-Royal,
long famed as the hatmakers' and milliners' district.
The firm's history spans almost two hundred years; records
of a milliner with the same name at this address on
Rue de Choiseul can be traced back to 1832. Some years later,
a haberdasher sold products referred to as *menue mercerie*:
all the essential accessories and paraphernalia for sewing
and embroidery. François Morin, a former financial executive,
purchased the notions store, followed by the milliner's
boutique, in the late 1990s. He was captivated by the history
of these places and acquired their historic inventories,
including a marvelous selection of ribbons, thread, felt,
veiling, trimmings, buttons, and lace. The expertise required
to produce such treasures had vanished by the end
of the twentieth century.
Today, the two shops face one another across the street,
each engaged in its particular activities: haberdashery on
one side, hats and passementerie on the other. The former,
which occupies a larger space, is a sewing sanctuary, and its
decor has remained unchanged. Shelves rise up to the ceiling,
the old counter runs the length of the store, and there
are numerous patinaed chests of drawers. Some of the wooden
display cabinets still bear the name of Cartier-Bresson:
a brand of thread that is now obsolete, but which made the
fortune of the famous photographer's family. Everything
contributes to the distinctive atmosphere that makes this
timeless place so appealing.
Whether customers come to purchase exquisite silk velvet
ribbons, felt fashioned from rabbit hair, or veiling of the
highest quality, they will discover that the inventory has
actually expanded over time. Stocks include thirty to forty
thousand buttons made of every imaginable material,
all arranged by color, as well as an impressive assortment
of grosgrain, ribbons, trimmings, and silk and cotton threads
in an infinitely varied array of colorful hues.

TOUT POUR LA ✹

Ultramod
MERCERIE
·
Ouvert
du Lundi au Vendredi
de 10 h à 18 h
·
Mercerie
Traditionnelle
Rubans Anciens
Passementerie
Boutons

MERCERIE

№ 117

COLORFUL THREADS

In French, the spool around which a thread
is wound is poetically known as its "soul"
(*âme*). Spools have existed since antiquity.
Originally fashioned from wood, they are now
made of cardboard or plastic. Their hollow
centers allow them to be slipped onto
a spindle.

MERCERIE
— ULTRAMOD —
BOUTONS EN TOUT GENRE
FILS DE SOIE À COUDRE

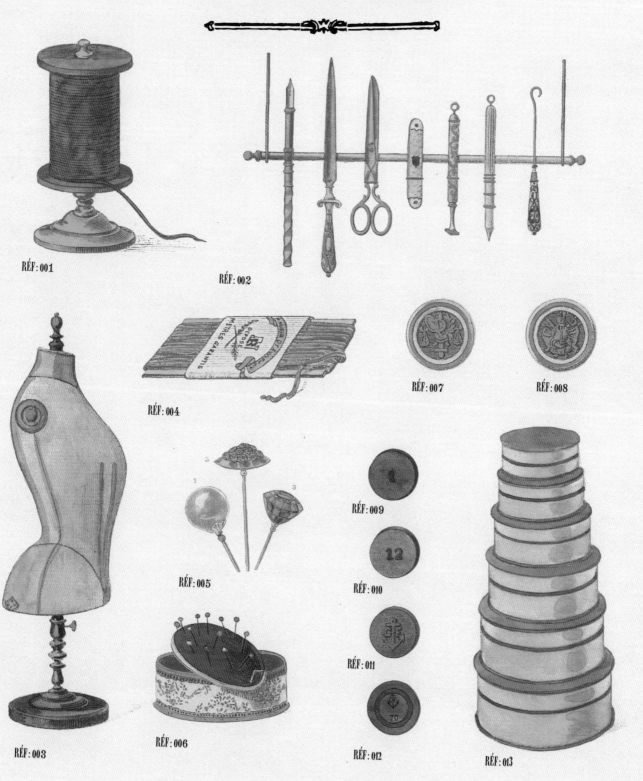

RÉF: 001

RÉF: 002

RÉF: 004

RÉF: 007

RÉF: 008

RÉF: 003

RÉF: 005

RÉF: 009

RÉF: 010

RÉF: 011

RÉF: 006

RÉF: 012

RÉF: 013

4, RUE DE CHOISEUL, PARIS 2ᴱ

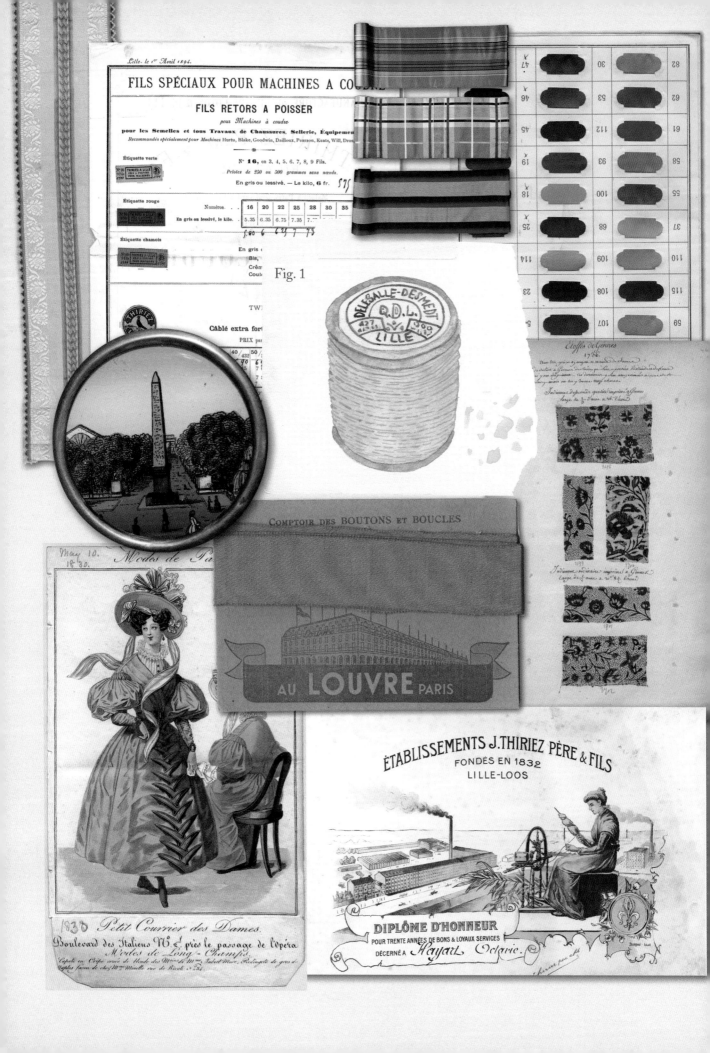

Lille, le 1er Avril 1894.

FILS SPÉCIAUX POUR MACHINES A COUDRE

FILS RETORS A POISSER

pour Machines à coudre

pour les Semelles et tous Travaux de Chaussures, Sellerie, Équipement

Recommandés spécialement pour Machines Hurtu, Blake, Goodwin, Dailloux, Pearson, Keats, Will, Dros...

Étiquette verte

N° **16**, en 3, 4, 5, 6, 7, 8, 9 Fils.

Pelotes de 250 ou 500 grammes sans nœuds.

En gris ou lessivé. — Le kilo, **6 fr.**

Étiquette rouge

Numéros. . .	16	20	22	25	28	30	35
En gris ou lessivé, le kilo	5.35	6.35	6.75	7.35	7...		

Étiquette chamois

En gris o...

Bis, ...

Crèm...

Coul...

Fig. 1

TW...

Câblé extra fort...

PRIX par...

Comptoir des Boutons et Boucles

AU **LOUVRE** PARIS

Modes de Pa...

May 10. 1830.

1830 Petit Courrier des Dames.

Boulevard des Italiens N° 9, près le passage de l'Opéra

Modes de Long-Champs

Capote en Crêpe ornée de ... des Mme & Mmes Aubert Maur, Redingote de gros de ...

Naples façon de chez M. Minette rue de Buck N° 75?

ÉTABLISSEMENTS J. THIRIEZ PÈRE & FILS

FONDÉS EN 1832

LILLE-LOOS

DIPLÔME D'HONNEUR

POUR TRENTE ANNÉES DE BONS & LOYAUX SERVICES

DÉCERNÉ A *Mayart Octavie*

Étoffes de Gênes 1786

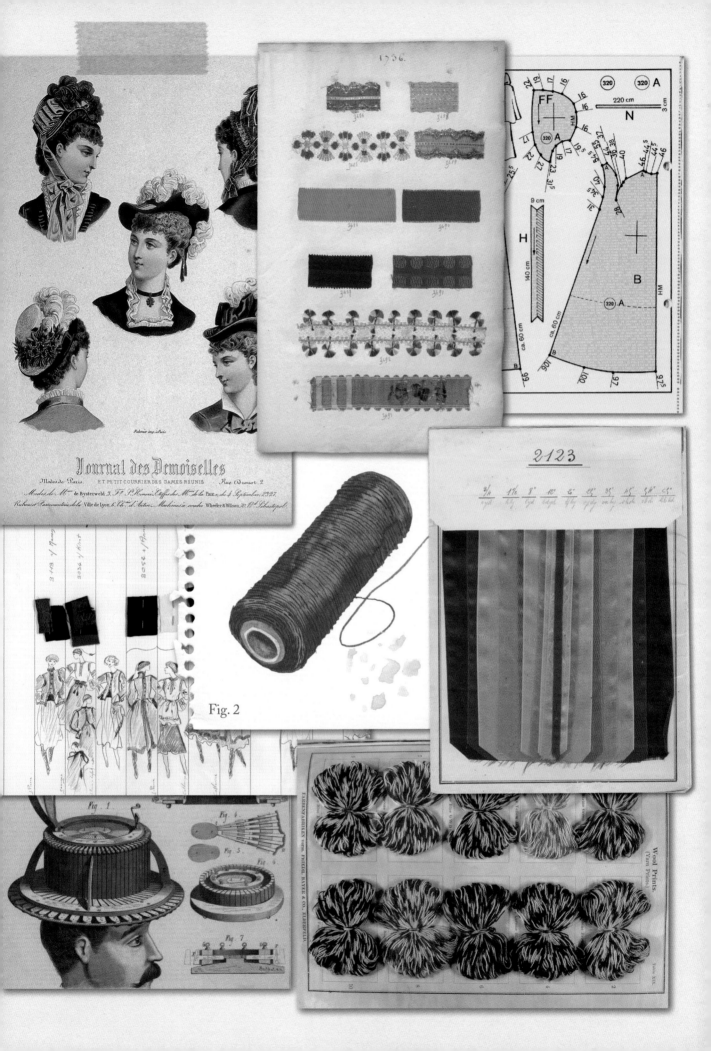

1786.

Journal des Demoiselles

Modes de Paris.   ET PETIT COURRIER DES DAMES RÉUNIS   Rue Drouot, 2

Modes de M.ᵐᵉ de Bysterweld, 3, F.ᵍ S.ᵗ Honoré, Etoffes des M.ᵈˢ de la Paix, r, de 4 Septembre, 2327.
Rubans et Passementerie de la Ville de Lyon, 6, Ch.ᵉᵉ d'Antin. Machines à coudre Wheeler & Wilson, 70 B.ᵈ Sébastopol.

320   320 A

N

220 cm

3 cm

9 cm

140 cm

H

B

ca. 60 cm

Fig. 2

2123

Fig. 1
Fig. 4
Fig. 5
Fig. 6
Fig. 7

Wool Prints.
(Garn Prints.)

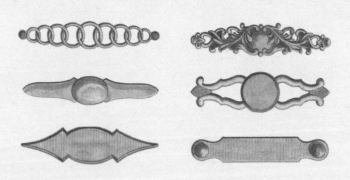

À LA PROVIDENCE

151 RUE DU FAUBOURG SAINT-ANTOINE — PARIS 11E

Not so long ago, Faubourg Saint-Antoine was the neighborhood of furniture makers. Nicolas Barbato, owner of this extraordinary hardware store founded in 1830, happily confesses that he carries "the soul of the faubourg within him." It is a soul that embraces the cabinetmakers, carpenters, gilders, carvers, bronze workers, and polishers, whose workshops were once ubiquitous in the neighborhood. À La Providence is a paean to the expertise of yesteryear. When Nicolas Barbato took over, he was determined to preserve the authenticity of the original furnishings: the wooden counter, walls covered with shelving, a cashier's station with glass partitions, and the front door that still displays the former owner's name spelled out in enameled lettering. Faithful to the early twentieth-century decor, he simply cleaned and rearranged the contents of the pigeonholes and storage chests, which contain thousands of carefully ordered items. When a client arrives with a special request, he leafs through the catalog: an incredible record of the past, in which each accessory has been painstakingly drawn by hand.
The store attracts customers from around the world, all in search of accessories and other articles, made specially in France, that can only be found here: bronze ornaments produced from the Louis XIII era until the 1930s, newel post finials made from sparkling faceted genuine crystal, and exquisite lock faceplates fashioned from mother-of-pearl or mammoth ivory. But you'll also find simpler accessories for the traditional locksmithing trade: levered door handles and hinges, doorstops, latches, and bolts, as well as screws for wood and metal.

The shop's interior has remained almost unchanged
for more than a century. The old stove is no longer in use,
but wooden cabinets still store thousands of items.

In this highly specialized hardware shop, visitors will find everything, from reproductions of seventeenth-century decorative accessories to engraved door handles or ornate armoire lock faceplates.

QUINCAILLERIE LECLERCQ
À LA PROVIDENCE

151 Rue du Faubourg Saint-Antoine, 75011 Paris

RÉF : 001

RÉF : 002

RÉF : 003

RÉF : 004

RÉF : 005

RÉF : 006

RÉF : 007

RÉF : 008

RÉF : 009

POUR LES DIMENSIONS ET LES QUALITÉS DIVERSES DES ARTICLES FIGURANT À CE CATALOGUE CONSULTEZ LE TARIF CI-JOINT.

G. W. Dasent Eagh

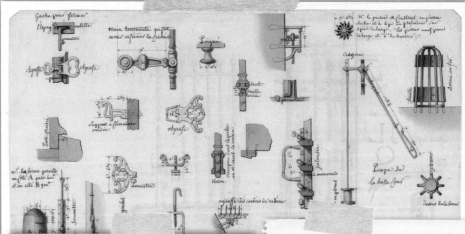

Fig. 1

A LA PROVIDENCE

QUINCAILLERIE LECLERCQ

S.A.R.L. CAPITAL 15.245 €

DAS EMPIRE-ORNAMENT

151, FAUBOURG SAINT-ANTOINE 75011 PARIS

TRAITÉ PRATIQUE
DE SERRURERIE

CONSTRUCTIONS EN FER
SERRURERIE D'ART

PAR
E. BARBEROT
ARCHITECTE

ORNÉ DE
870 figures
DANS LE TEXTE

PARIS
LIBRAIRIE POLYTECHNIQUE, BAUDRY ET Cᵉ, ÉDITEURS
15, RUE DES SAINTS-PÈRES, 15
MAISON À LIÈGE, RUE LAMBERT-CRÉCOUR, 19

1888
Tous droits réservés.

NOTICE
SUR LA

SERRURERIE

DE PICARDIE

PAR R. Brice

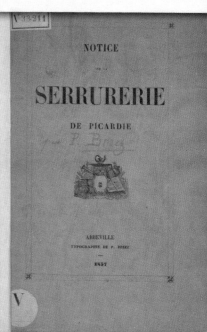

ABBEVILLE
TYPOGRAPHIE DE P. BRIEZ

1857

A D

PL. 16

DAS EMPIRE-ORNAMENT

Tafel 9

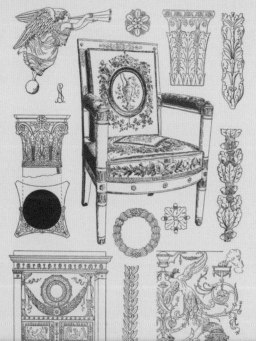

Fig. 2

Gauthier, 2, Rue Saint-Antoine

KEY TO JERRY'S CELL

In 1851 what is now known as the Jerry Rescue Building was called The Journal Building, and the Police Office was in it, at No. 2 Clinton Street. There Jerry was taken after his recapture.

FÉAU & CIE

The Ternes district of Paris was still a village among fields
in 1875. The entrepreneur Charles Fournier decided to locate
his new workshop there because it was close to the Plaine
Monceau, a neighborhood frequented by the rich and powerful.
These were the clients who purchased Fournier's antique wood
paneling to adorn the walls of their private residences.
The grandfather of the current owner, Guillaume Féau,
purchased the business in 1953. Over the decades, three
generations of the Féau family—decorators with a keen eye
for antiques—have tirelessly frequented auction houses,
gradually accumulating an impressive collection of
incomparable pieces. The entire history of French decor from
the seventeenth to the twentieth centuries is represented
here, in the nooks and crannies of this vast labyrinth.
It extends beneath a monumental steel and glass cupola, reminiscent
of one of Eiffel's lofty structures. Wainscoting, doors, trompe-
l'oeil works, and carved panels highlighted with gilt or painted
decorations are displayed, as well as mirrors, mantelpieces,
fountains, plasterwork, drawings, and engravings. It is an
authentic living museum of French decorative heritage. There is
much to marvel at, from a rococo panel, possibly stripped from
the Château de Versailles, to columns finely etched with daisies,
created in 1920 by eminent designer Armand-Albert Rateau for
Jeanne Lanvin's town house.
The business shifted its focus in the 1990s and ceased the sale of
antiques, with rare exceptions made for a few museums, foundations,
and knowledgeable collectors. Féau & Cie now supplies the most
prominent designers, and it works on about a hundred projects
annually. Scrupulously preserved antiques serve as models for
reproductions, created in their own workshops and destined for
luxurious residences throughout the world.

This extraordinary monumental fountain, which also served
as a boot scraper, was presented by François Blanc, founder
of the Société des Bains de Mer de Monaco, to his son-in-law
Prince Radziwiłł. The work is by Charles Cordier and animal
sculptor Auguste Caïn.

BOISERIES
FÉAU & CIE
AU 9, RUE LAUGIER
75017 PARIS

RÉF: 166

RÉF: 167

RÉF: 168

RÉF: 174

RÉF: 169

RÉF: 170

RÉF: 171

RÉF: 172

Fig. 166. — Assemblage à queue-d'aronde recouverte.

Fig. 167. — Assemblage d'onglet à clef.

Fig. 168. — Assemblage d'onglet à tenon et mortaise.

11. Assemblage d'onglet avec clef (**fig. 167**).	16. **Assemblage** d'un jet d'eau de croisée.
12. — d'onglet à tenon et mortaise (**fig. 168**).	17. — d'un montant de porte avec panneau et traverse.
13. — à enfourchement simple.	
14. — à double enfourchement.	18. — d'un montant de porte à grand cadre avec panneau.
15. — d'un petit bois de croisée.	

La collection de 18 modèles d'assemblage de menuiserie.............. 26 »

Chaque modèle séparément du n° 1 à 14................................ 2 »

— — du n° 15 à 17................................ 2 25

du n° 18................................ 3 »

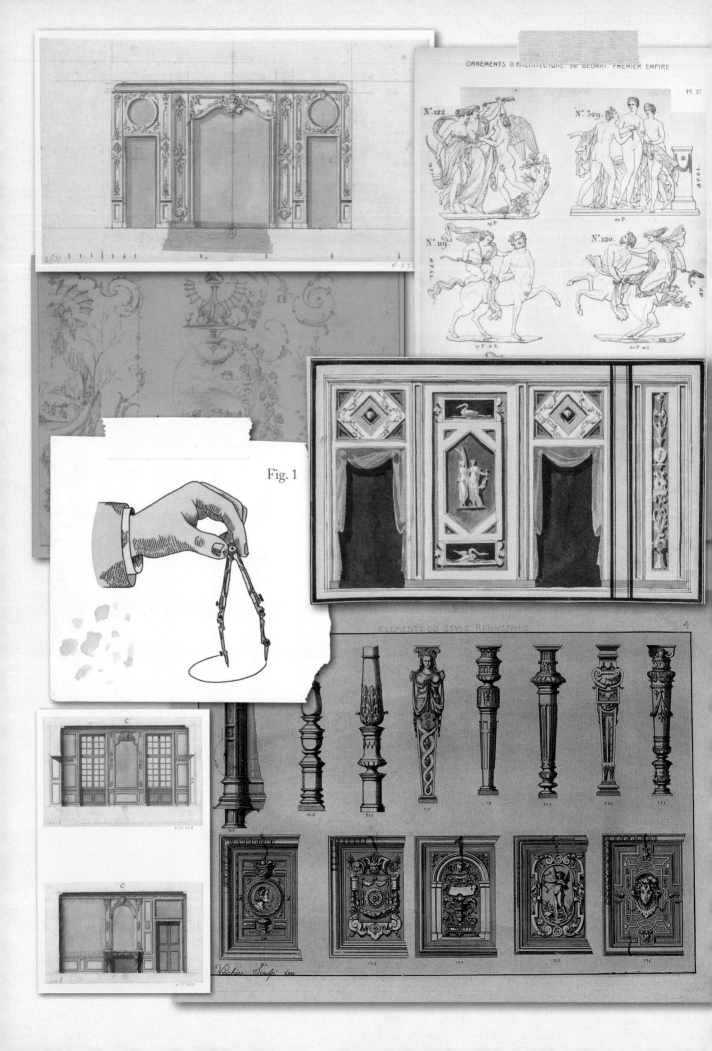

ORNEMENTS D'ARCHITECTURE, par BEUNAT, PREMIER EMPIRE

Pl. 27

N° 122.

N° 329.

N° 119.

N° 120.

Fig. 1

ELEMENTS DU STYLE RENAISSANCE

4

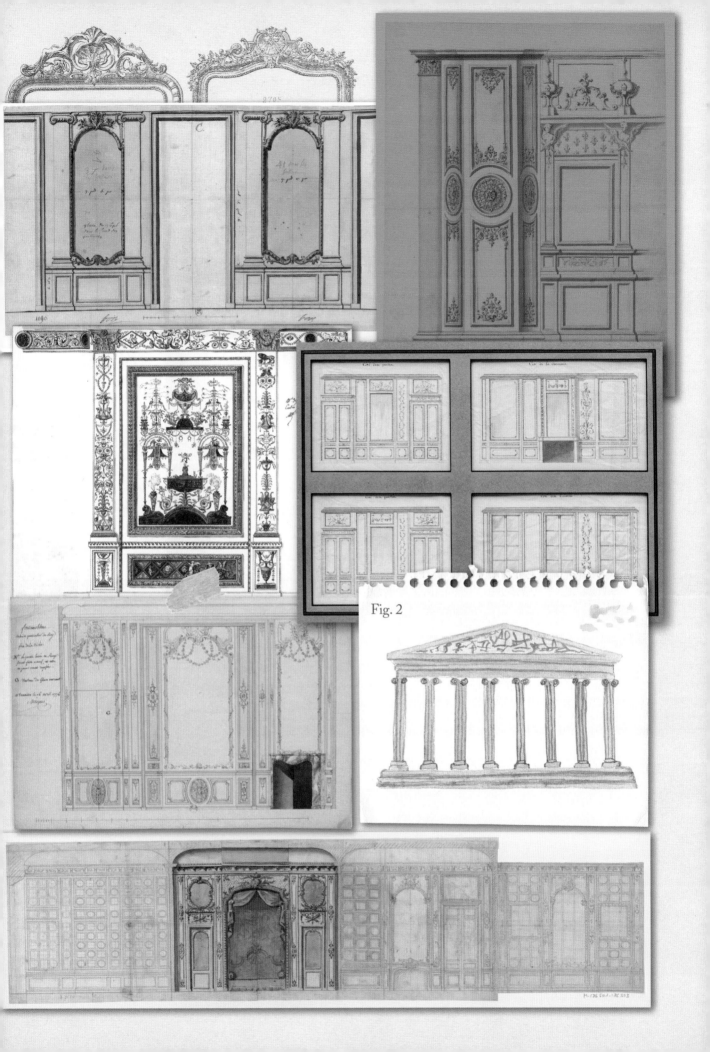

Fig. 2

SOUBRIER

Maison Soubrier has been owned by the same family for over two hundred years. The firm originally produced period furniture, before moving into antique dealing. Louis Soubrier, the current owner, spent years visiting auction houses to indulge his passion for historic furnishings and beautiful objects, which he then sold to a few fortunate clients.
He vividly recalls one of his all-time favorites: an imposing bronze aquamanile—a water ewer or jug, often in the shape of an animal—dating from the Renaissance, which was extremely rare and far too costly to purchase. He was given a second chance to buy it a few years later, as its age had been reassessed downward, along with its price.
In recent years, the firm has focused exclusively on rentals. This extraordinary destination is a well-kept secret that's open only to the trade, and attracts professional designers, decorators, and stylists from film, theater, and television. Once past its portals, the visitor enters a courtyard and encounters two marble sphinxes flanking the entrance.
Inside, an antique elevator paneled with original wainscoting, which dates back to 1900, moves between the three floors at a stately pace. The unparalled collection extends over 32,000 square feet (3,000 m²). It is meticulously organized by category, and everything on show is available for rent, from a Napoleon III-era presidential desk from the Élysée Palace, to an immense baroque mirror decorated with horns, or a copper deep-sea diver's helmet; curiously, the most frequently borrowed piece in the catalog is a 1920s cheval glass (full-length mirror). This accumulation of antique furniture, paintings, and objects—reminiscent of a vast cabinet of curiosities—is imbued with an indefinable scent that mingles dust, polished wood, and old documents, calling to mind the attic of a charming provincial home.

FURNITURE

Introduced around 1725, the *bergère*
armchair features gently curved
lines. The upholstered back, padded
armrests, and soft seat cushion are
an invitation to relax.

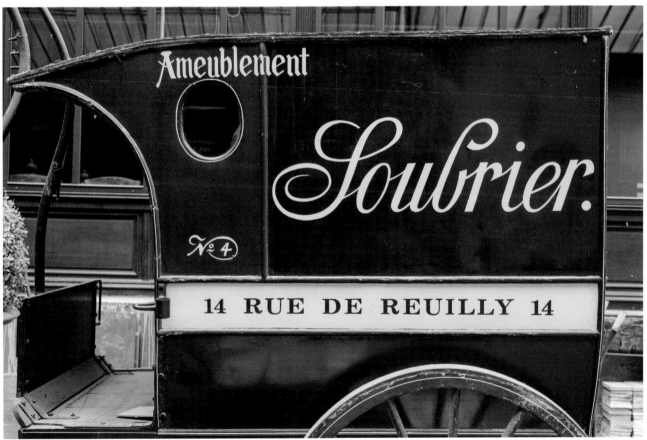

AMEUBLEMENT
SOUBRIER
14, RUE DE REUILLY
PARIS

RÉF: 001

RÉF: 002

RÉF: 003

RÉF: 004

RÉF: 005

RÉF: 006

Modèle Nᵒ 55 avec 9 tiroirs pour dessins de 0.65 × 0.50			165 - »
Modèle Nᵒ 58 — — 0.85 × 0.65			280 »
Modèle Nᵒ 61 — — 1.14 × 0.80			355 »

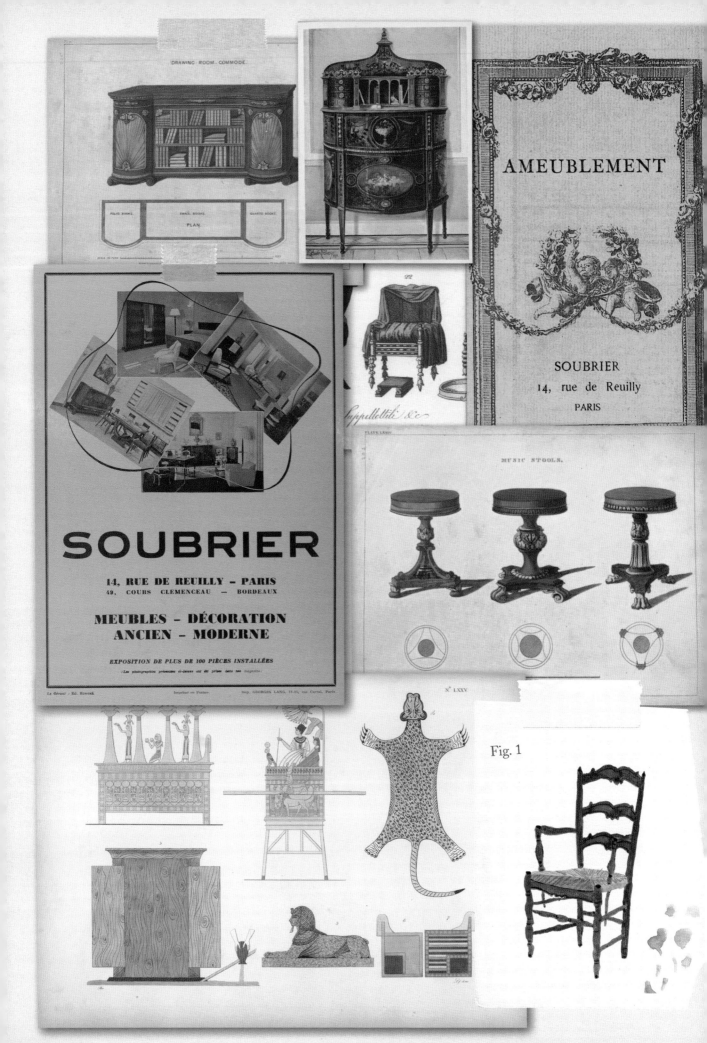

DRAWING ROOM COMMODE.

PLAN.

AMEUBLEMENT

SOUBRIER
14, rue de Reuilly
PARIS

MUSIC STOOLS.

SOUBRIER

14, RUE DE REUILLY — PARIS
49, COURS CLEMENCEAU — BORDEAUX

MEUBLES – DÉCORATION
ANCIEN – MODERNE

EXPOSITION DE PLUS DE 100 PIÈCES INSTALLÉES

Fig. 1

MOBILIER DÉCORATION

REVUE MENSUELLE
DES
ARTS DÉCORATIFS
APPLIQUÉS
ET DE
L'ARCHITECTURE
MODERNE

1939
2

ÉDITIONS EDMOND HONORÉ
76, AVENUE DE SUFFREN — PARIS (XVᵉ)
1ᵉ ANNÉE

Février   France: Prix 12 fr.

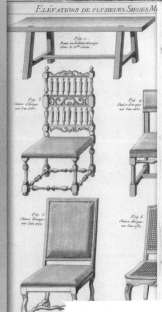

Fig. 2

AMEUBLEMENT

SOUBRIER

14, Rue de Reuilly, Paris.

IDEM PARIS

49 RUE DU MONTPARNASSE — PARIS 14E

In 1881, the printer Eugène Dufrenoy selected the site
at 49 Rue du Montparnasse to construct a building to house
his lithographic press. Later, he extended the workshop,
adding a second building that was connected to the first
by a little courtyard beneath a glass roof, to create a space
that spanned 15,000 square feet (1,400 m²).
Between 1930 and 1970, the company printed maps. In 1976,
the famous printer Fernand Mourlot moved in. Mourlot,
a lithographic master printer, worked with the greatest
artists of his time: Matisse, Picasso, Miró, Dubuffet, Braque,
Chagall, Giacometti, Léger, Cocteau, and Calder, among others.
A weighty lithographic stone still featuring the evocative
outline of a drawing by Picasso bears witness to this
illustrious past.
In 1997, Patrice Forest-art editor for conceptualist
artists including Miquel Barceló, Gérard Garouste,
and Jean-Michel Alberola-acquired "this enormous vessel
anchored in Montparnasse," as he called it. He changed nothing
in the historic workshop, keeping it just as it had been
in the 1880s. Looking up at the ceiling, visitors can see
the system of belts and pulleys of drive shafts activated
by a steam engine, which powers the old Voirin and Marinoni
presses still in operation today. This place is the stuff
of legend yet is in constant creative evolution.
Continuity is assured by young printers and contemporary
artists, such as JR, who are captivated by the beauty and
atmosphere of the workshop, and by the power of the colossal
machines that have survived through the years. David Lynch
nicknamed the largest of them Moby Dick, after Herman
Melville's great white whale. Fascinated by the vast presses
and the magic of the lithographic stones, Lynch often visits
the atelier when staying in Paris. It even features in an episode
of his series *Twin Peaks*, with Monica Bellucci, and he has also
directed a short black-and-white documentary on Idem Paris.

№166

Menton

Festival de Musique de Chambre

18 NOVEMBRE - 24 DECEMBRE 1975

Cathelin

GALERIE DE PARIS
14 Place François Ier   Peintures

GALERIE YOSHII
8 Avenue Matignon   Aquarelles

GALERIE GUIOT
18 Avenue Matignon   Lithographies
                              Tapisseries

Musée National
Message Biblique
Marc Chagall

Nice

PLACE
DU
CONCORDE

roger bézombes

France EUROPE

GH
AUX

VRIL-MAI 1960
MEDI DE 10 H. 30 A 22 HEURES

ANDRÉ BRASILIER

GALERIE DES CHAUDRONNIERS
10-12, RUE DES CHAUDRONNIERS · GENÈVE · 9 JUIN · 31 AOÛT 1981

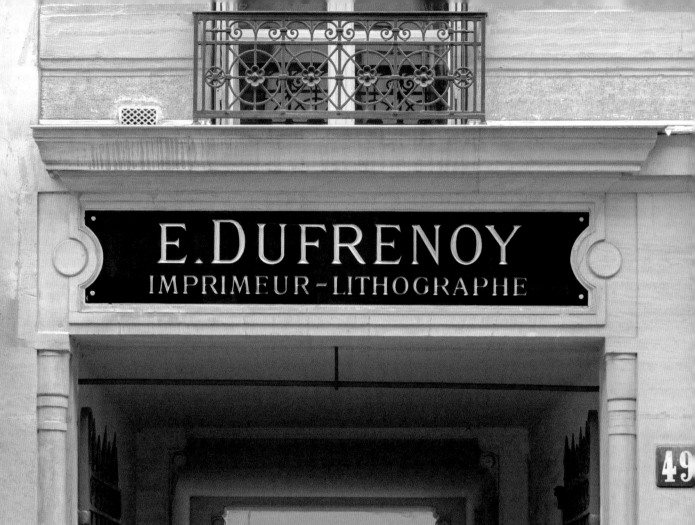

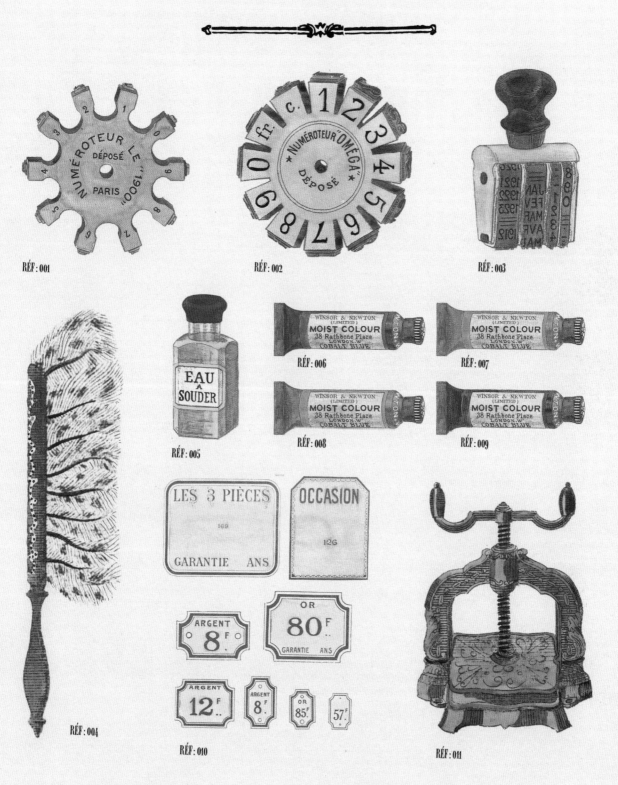

IMPRIMEUR - LITHOGRAPHE
IDEM
ANCIEN ÉTABLISSᵀ MOURLOT

RÉF : 001

RÉF : 002

RÉF : 003

RÉF : 005

RÉF : 006

RÉF : 007

RÉF : 008

RÉF : 009

RÉF : 004

RÉF : 010

RÉF : 011

49 RUE DU MONTPARNASSE, PARIS XIVᴱ

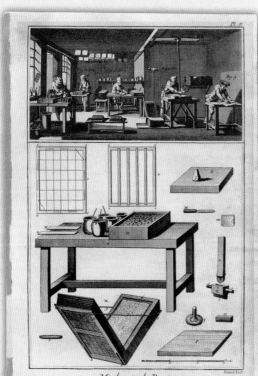

Marbreur de Papier.

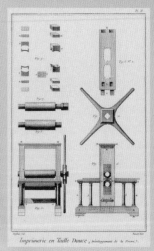

Imprimerie en Taille Douce, développement de la Presse.

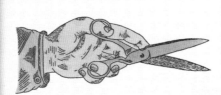

Bonne Chance
à ~ Fernand

Le 18 rue de Chabrol
c'est une usine
d'aristocrates
c'est le royaume
de l'artisanat ~ C'est
l'ordre du désordre
c'est la France de
Balzac ~ c'est ce
qu'on tremble de voir
disparaître
Jean Cocteau
* 1960

Chargé d'adresse

Mourlot *

Fig. 1

Le Testament
d'Orphée

Jean Cocteau

*

MARINONI VOIRIN   PARIS

528

HOMMAGE A FERNAND MOURLOT

יובל לסדנת מורלו, פאריס
תערוכת הדפסי-אבן של אמני מופת אירופיים במאה העשרים

L'ATELIER MOURLOT DE PARIS
lithographies des grands maîtres de l'art moderne

FERNAND MOURLOT

CHAGALL
LITHOGRAPH

1957-1962

VERLAG ANDRÉ SAURET
MONTE CARLO

HOMMAGE A FERNAND MOURLOT

SENNELIER

It is impossible to imagine a better location: Maison
Sennelier is situated on the Quai Voltaire, across from
the Musée du Louvre, on a site first owned by a paint merchant
established in the eighteenth century. It has been owned
by the same family since 1887.
Sophie Sennelier, the founder's great-granddaughter, recalls
her ancestor's story. Trained as a chemist, Gustave Sennelier
began producing colors for artists, in the form of oil
paints, watercolors, and pastels. Before the invention of the
grinder, he crushed the pigments himself by hand in a mortar.
It was Cézanne who urged Sennelier to broaden the palette of
colors he was offering. Degas also patronized this renowned
establishment and purchased his famous soft pastels here.
Later, Picasso, Sonia and Robert Delaunay, and Nicolas de
Staël were clients. David Hockney is a regular these days.
The shop's façade has remained unaltered since the nineteenth
century. The interior is filled with old counters, glass
cabinets, and oak furnishings that lend their charm to the
cavernous treasure trove. Oil paint, specially-made honey-
based watercolors, dry and soft pastels in hundreds of
different tones, gouaches, acrylics, and colored inks are
organized next to pencils, brushes of all sizes, notebooks,
and sketch pads aplenty—more than thirty-five thousand
items in all. The upstairs is devoted to paper of all sorts,
produced from cotton, sisal, bamboo, and papyrus. Some types
are made in France; others are imported from farther afield,
including China, Mexico, Thailand, India, Egypt, Korea,
and Nepal. Their grains range from fine to rough, and some
are encrusted with straw, moss, rice, mother-of-pearl,
or coral, like the brilliant "moon papers" from Vietnam.
Everything displayed here is an inspiration to paint or draw.
A simple sketchbook and a box of watercolors are all you need
to get started.

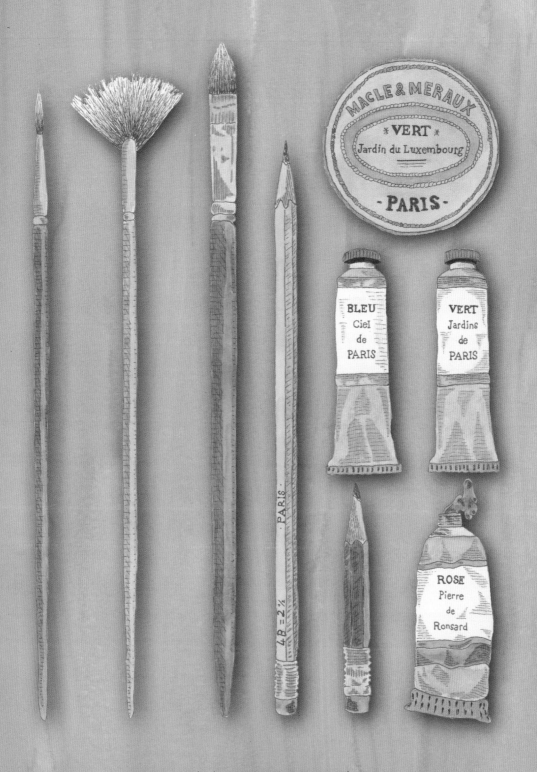

ART SUPPLIES

In 1841, the American artist John Goffe Rand invented a flexible tin tube containing ready-to-use paint. The container could be closed with a resealable clip. This practical packaging made paint simple to use and easy to transport.

207 CENDRE BLEU   006 BLEU PÂLE   003 BLEU CÉRULÉUM   016 GRIS VERT   046 VERT OLIVE

205 VERT MOUSSE   042 VERT CINABRE JAUNE   045 VERT MOYEN   044 VERT ÉMERAUDE   125 PERLE

230 ROSE INDIEN   025 OCRE DE CHAIR   232 FEUILLE MORTE   090 ORANGE DE CHINE   092 BRUN DE MADÈRE

091 TITANE BUFF   243 TERRE OMBRIA   093 BRUN SENNELIER CLAIR   036 TERRE DE SIENNE BRULÉE   034 TERRE D'OMBRE BRULE

144 OR RICHE   132 PERLE DORÉE   026 OCRE JAUNE   037 TERRE SIENNE NATUR.   035 TERRE D'OMBRE NATUR

001 BLANC   014 GRIS PÂLE   012 GRIS FONCÉ   096 GRIS DE PAYNE   025 NOIR

001 BLANC   123 BLEU TRANSPARENT   124   135   023 NOIR

PASTEL à L'HUILE GÉANT

13,21€

ELS A L'HUILE
TELIER"

1,62€

SENNELIER
3, Quai Voltaire
PARIS

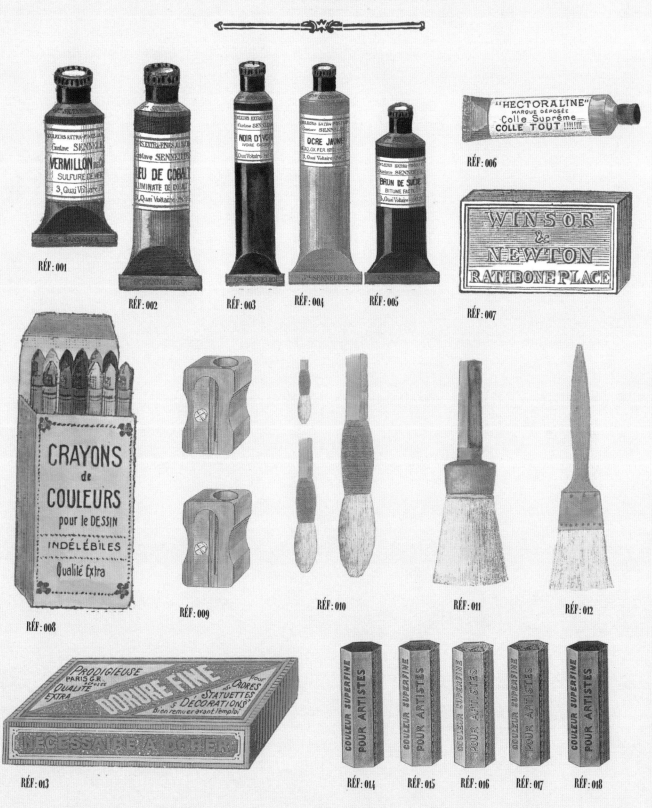

RÉF: 001

RÉF: 002

RÉF: 003

RÉF: 004

RÉF: 005

RÉF: 006

RÉF: 007

RÉF: 008

RÉF: 009

RÉF: 010

RÉF: 011

RÉF: 012

RÉF: 013

RÉF: 014

RÉF: 015

RÉF: 016

RÉF: 017

RÉF: 018

FABRICANT DE COULEURS FINES ET MATÉRIEL POUR ARTISTES.

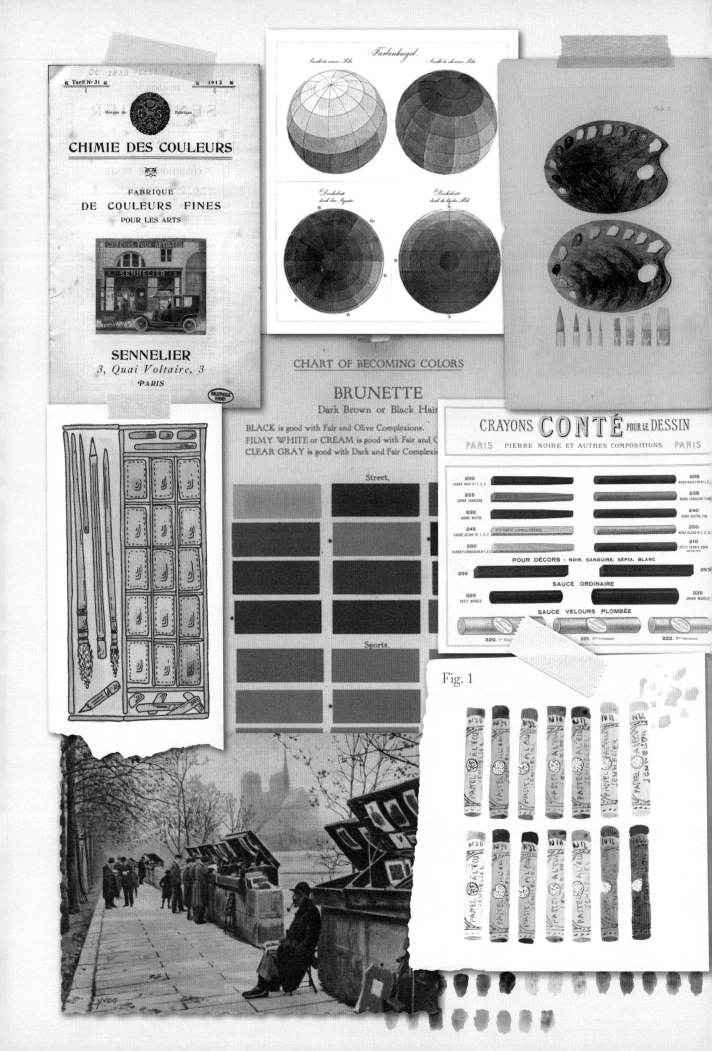

Fig. 2

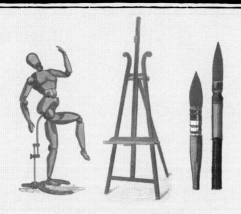

ACADÉMIE DE LA G^{DE} CHAUMIÈRE

14 RUE DE LA GRANDE CHAUMIÈRE — PARIS 6^E

The Académie de la Grande Chaumière-the legendary studio
of artistic Montparnasse-was established in 1904. Students
have always enrolled here to practice their art freely,
without constraints. Teaching is based on the nude model;
a simple screen shields them from prying eyes as they undress,
before assuming a pose. The nudes may be depicted in pencil,
charcoal, oil paint, acrylic, or watercolor-every medium is
allowed. Dozens of pictures covering the walls attest to
diverse sources of inspiration.
The ancient woodstove no longer crackles, but it still imposes
its presence in the studio, like a large cast-iron sculpture.
Old stools of various sizes are piled in the corners,
and easels bearing the traces of decades of paint are stacked
against the walls. Light streams in through huge windows
to illuminate the crumbling walls, whose surfaces are strewn
with mildew markings reminiscent of a Jackson Pollock artwork.
Repainting them would be deemed a sacrilege by those
who frequent the studio now. The students cleave loyally
to the atmosphere of authenticity-a legacy of years past.
The ghosts of generations of famous sculptors and painters
haunt the space. Antoine Bourdelle and Ossip Zadkine
taught sculpture here, and the very greatest artists
passed through its halls: Amedeo Modigliani, Marc Chagall,
Alberto Giacometti, Louise Bourgeois, Joan Miró, Bernard
Buffet, Fernand Léger, Zao Wou-Ki, Tsuguharu Foujita, and
Alexander Calder, to name but a few. A rather shy young man,
determined to pursue a career in painting, also spent time
at the academy; in those days, he went by the name of Lucien
Ginsburg. He later turned to music and assumed the stage name
that made him a legend: Serge Gainsbourg.

SCULPTURE
Atelier
ROBERT WLERICK

SCULPTURE
Atelier O. ZADKINE

PEINTURE
Atelier Yves BRAYER

PEINTURE
Atelier Pierre JEROME

PEINTURE
Atelier René ARTOZOUL

☼ ACADÉMIE ☼
DE LA
GRANDE CHAUMIÈRE
FONDÉE EN 1904

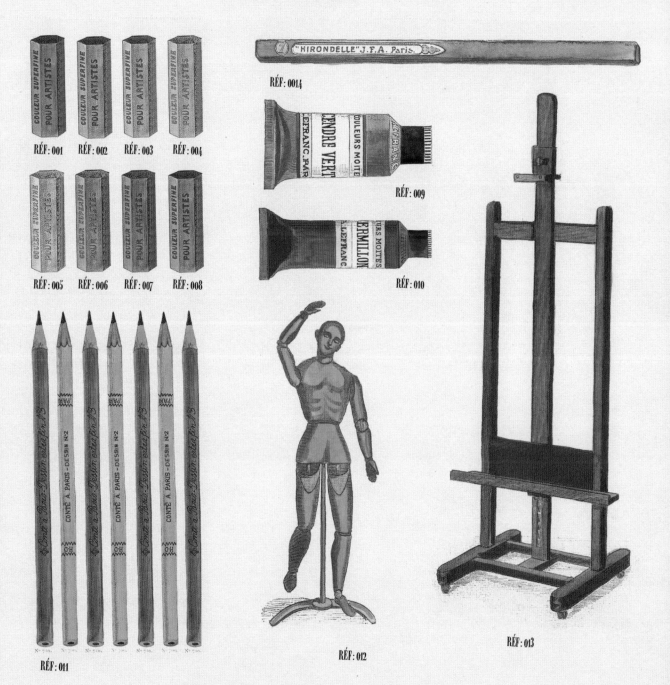

RÉF: 001   RÉF: 002   RÉF: 003   RÉF: 004

RÉF: 005   RÉF: 006   RÉF: 007   RÉF: 008

RÉF: 0014

RÉF: 009

RÉF: 010

RÉF: 011

RÉF: 012

RÉF: 013

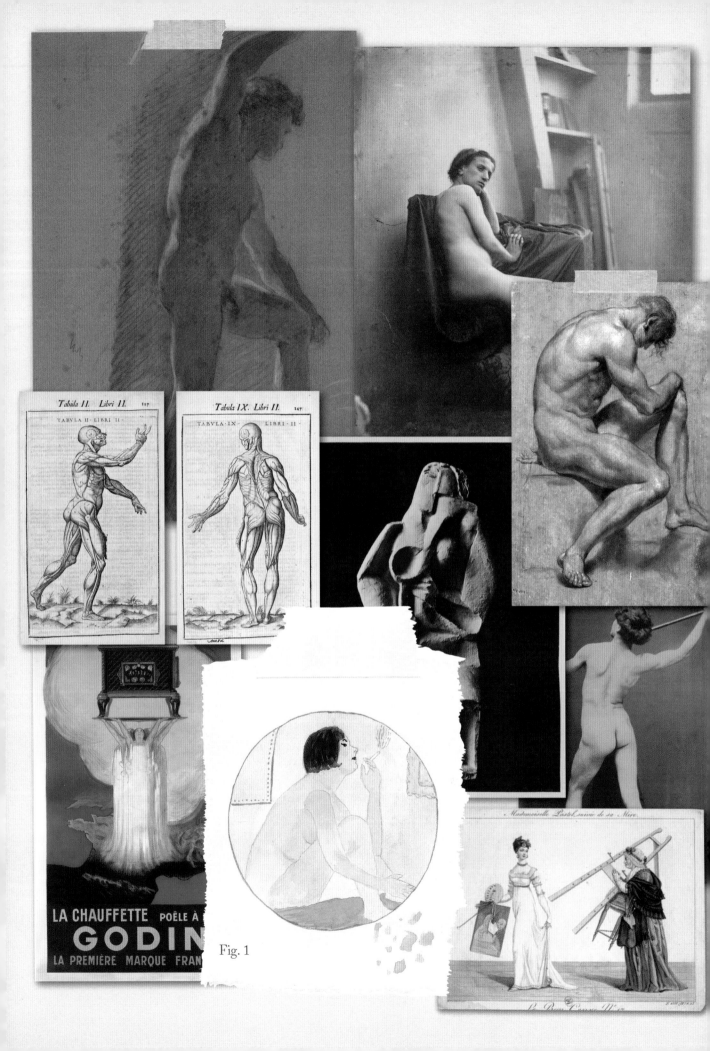

Fig. 1

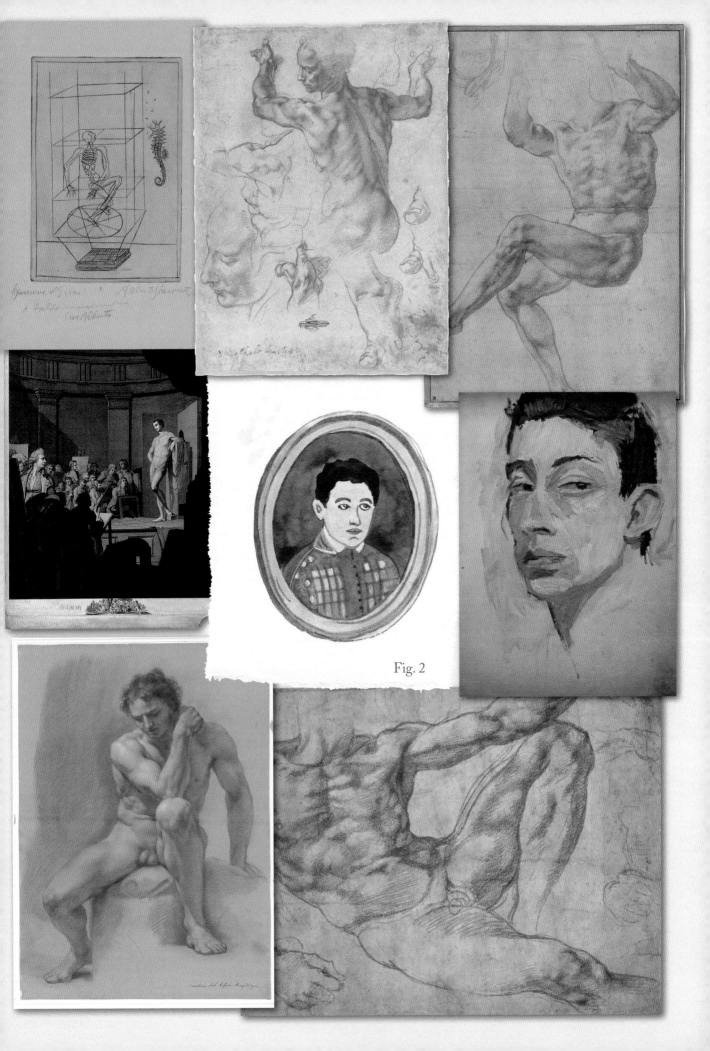

Fig. 2

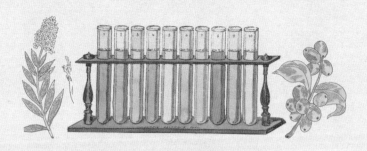

HERBORISTERIE DE LA PLACE CLICHY

87 RUE D'AMSTERDAM — PARIS 8ᴱ

Established in 1880, this marvelous herbalist's shop embodies
the survival of historic Paris with its period signage,
gold lettering on a black background, and original façade
painted a pretty shade of yellow. Yet it came close to
oblivion when a law was passed in 1941 that abolished the
qualifying diploma for herbalists, consigning the sale of
medicinal plants and other traditional remedies (known as
herbes de bonne femme, a variant of the Latin expression *bona
fama*, meaning "of good repute") to licensed pharmacists only.
Fortunately, that's no longer the case, and shoppers can still
go to 87 Rue d'Amsterdam to purchase plants and custom-made
tisanes, infusions, and other decoctions.
These proprietary blends are packaged in white paper sacks,
carefully labeled by hand, and displayed in attractive
baskets. They exude an intense fragrance that pervades amid
the old wooden shelves, the traditional glass or painted
porcelain apothecary jars, and the quaint copper beam scale.
There is a remedy here for every minor ailment, from bad
digestion or circulatory problems, to headaches, insomnia,
and respiratory difficulties. Hundreds of preparations
are on offer. If suffering from a hangover, you'll want
the tisane that treats swollen, sluggish livers. For glowing
skin, try the specially refined oils, such as nourishing wheat
germ, or calendula, which is effective for minor irritations.
For hair, turn to time-honored traditional treatments like
shea and jojoba.
This herbalist's boutique also proposes dried flowers
and herbs for making potpourris, which can be placed
throughout the home for a distinctive fragrance. Combine
the rapturous scent of dried damask rosebuds with a touch
of lemon verbena, lavender, or mint; scatter over dried
marigold and cornflower petals for a little color contrast;
and add a few drops of your favorite essential oil, to create
your very own personalized potpourri with all-natural scents.

GELSEMIUM

HERBIER

AMOUR

VÉRITABLE

PLANTS

Leaves, flowers, roots, bark,
and seeds can all be used in the
preparation of tisanes, infusions,
pomades, creams, ointments,
and beneficial oils.

87 ✱ HERBORISTERIE

HERBORISTERIE

Depuis 1880

Tisanes . Préparations . Conseils

E LA PLACE CLICHY * 87

IL Y A
DES
MOMENTS
OÙ TOUT
RÉUSSIT
IL NE FAUT PAS
S'INQUIÉTER.
ÇA
PASSE

HERBORISTERIE   HERBORISTERIE

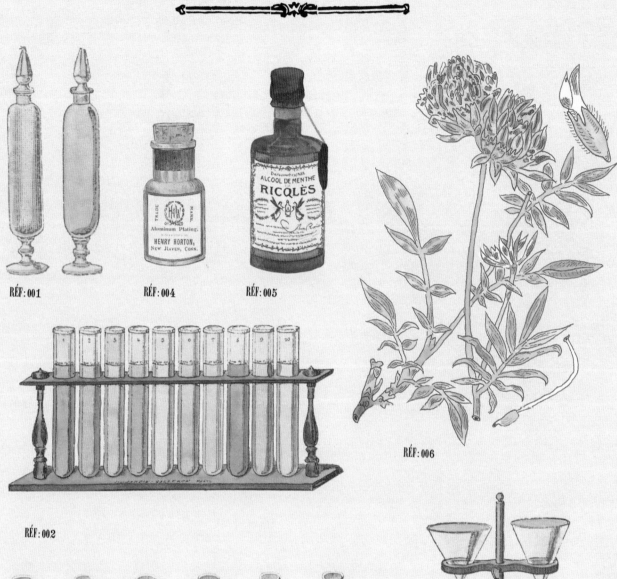

RÉF: 001

RÉF: 004

RÉF: 005

RÉF: 006

RÉF: 002

RÉF: 003

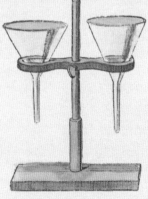

RÉF: 007

Schizanthus pinnatus, HUMBLE.

PHILIPPE GILLE

L'Herbier

POÉSIES

PARIS
ALPHONSE LEMERRE, ÉDITEUR
27-31, PASSAGE CHOISEUL, 27-31

M DCCC LXXXVII

Prunus armeniaca. Linn. Labricotier commun.

Eucalyptus globulus

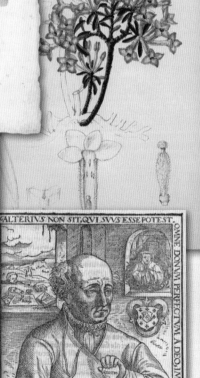

ALTERIVS NON SIT, QVI SVVS ESSE POTEST.

OMNE DONVM PERFECTVM A DEO, IMPERE A DIABO

AVREOLVS PHILIPPVS THEOPHRASTVS

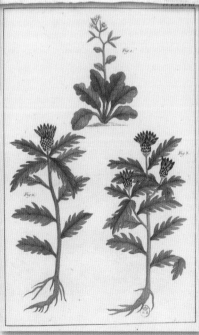

HERBIER

OU COLLECTION

DES PLANTES MEDICINALES

DE LA CHINE

D'après un Manuscrit peint et unique
qui se trouve dans la Bibliotheque
de l'Empereur de la Chine.

POUR SERVIR DE SUITTE

AUX PLANCHES ENLUMINÉES ET NON ENLUMINÉES

D'HISTOIRE NATURELLE

et à la Collection des Fleurs

qui se cultivent dans les Jardins de la Chine et de l'Europe.

Dirigé par les Soins
de Mr. Buchoz, Médecin de Monsieur.

A PARIS.

Chez L'Auteur rue de la Harpe vis-à-vis celle de Richelieu-Sorbonne.

1781.

De
WONDEREN GODS
in de
minst-geachte
SCHEPSELEN.

J. C. SEPP excudit.

Fig. 1

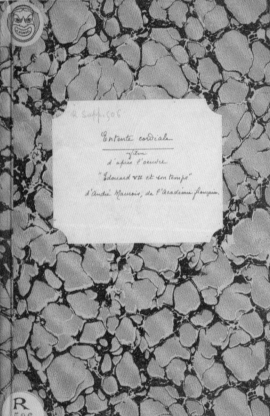

FORMULAIRE

DE

L'HERBORISTERIE

CONTENANT

Étude générale du végétal au point de vue
thérapeutique — Récolte — Conservation — Mise
en valeur des principes médicaux — Adjuvants et
incomp...

Dr S.-E. MAURIN

QUASSIA

ANIS VERTS

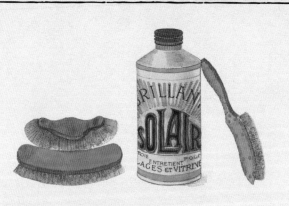

PRODUITS D'ANTAN

10 RUE SAINT-BERNARD — PARIS 11^{E}

There are still some places on Faubourg Saint-Antoine
that preserve the memory of workers and artisans who labored
here long ago. That is certainly the case with this unique
emporium of household products, which has been in operation
for nearly a century. The signage recalls its historic
mission: "Specialties for marble workers and cabinetmakers."
The original decor still remains, with wooden furnishings
and racks holding a plethora of products for professionals
and knowledgeable do-it-yourselfers.
Nathalie Lefebvre, who bought the store "out of passion"
in 2014, prides herself on stocking thousands of products
to maintain, restore, strip, polish, buff, and bring a shine
to materials including wood, marble, leather, stone, concrete,
and all kinds of metal—from bronze or steel to copper or
brass. Some of her specialties captivate novices, such as
Eau Japonaise, "the concoction that restores all types of
varnishes and bronzes"; this old recipe has been treasured
by workers in the neighborhood since it was created in
1889. And then there is jade oil, which is used to protect
metals from oxidation. Other offerings include hematite
and tourmaline, which have nothing to do with semiprecious
gems; they are liquids used to color metals with a variety
of tints, including black, copper, and blue. One of the
shop's most popular products is Majoline: a beauty cream for
every type of metal, which works equally well on crystal and
precious stones. Dozens of brushes for every imaginable use are
displayed behind the cash register, with bristles fashioned
from strands of silk, metal, nylon, and even goose feathers.
Nathalie Lefebvre also plans to expand her selection of natural
housekeeping products to make at home, particularly washing
powders and soaps. This historic emporium is entering a new era.

DOUCINE

FOURNEAU

VIELON

BIJOUX

PRODUCTS OF YESTERYEAR

These cleaning products and tools,
tried and tested over generations,
are unequalled for scrubbing,
shining, polishing, and patinating
all kinds of materials.

* PRODUITS D'ANTAN *

ENTRETIEN ET RÉNOVATION DES MEUBLES,
OBJETS D'ART ET SOLS

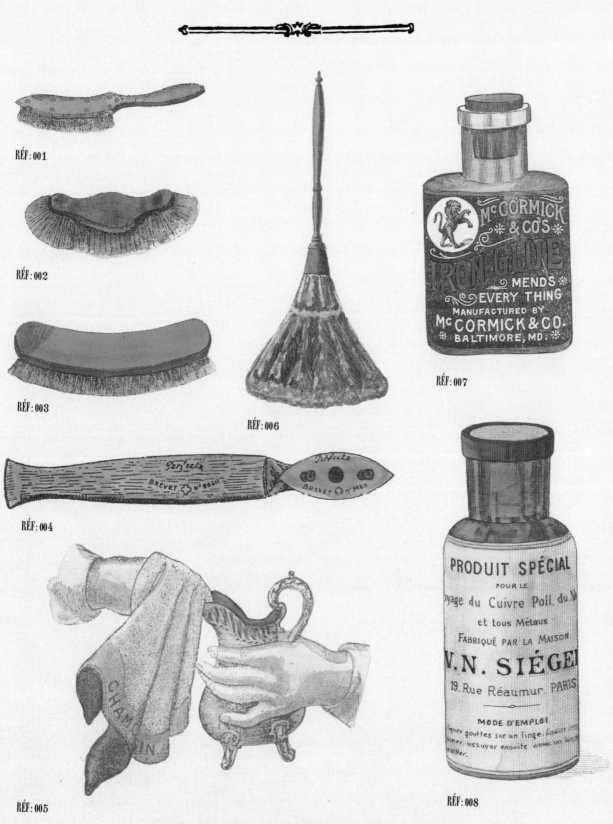

RÉF: 001

RÉF: 002

RÉF: 003

RÉF: 006

RÉF: 007

RÉF: 004

RÉF: 005

RÉF: 008

10, RUE SAINT BERNARD — 75011 PARIS

Fig. 1

le beau MENUISIER ou encore un Copeau
HISTORIETTE

D'après nature pour l'instruction de la jeunesse. Bilder zum Anschauungs Unterricht für die Jugend.

MENUISIER.

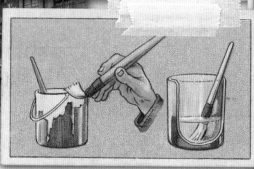

Habit de Menuisier Ebeniste.

ENCAUSTIQUE
BiKiNi
l'essence de térébenthine

Sans effort
tout brille !

SAVON
DE
MARSEILLE

Carpenter.

Bricklayer.

Farrier

Coachm

Fig. 2

DEMANDEZ
le Savon Pur
"LE SAPIN"
72%

persil
PRODUIT FRANÇAIS
LAVE TOUT TOUT SEUL

Engraver.

House Painter.

Plumber.

Waggoner.

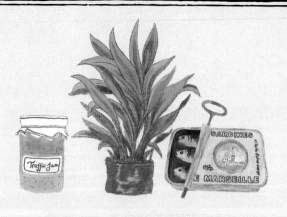

GRAINETERIE DU MARCHÉ

8 PLACE D'ALIGRE — PARIS 12ᴱ

Place d'Aligre has been the location of the largest food market in Paris for centuries. It is famed for its covered market, its fruit and vegetable stalls, and the antique stands that attract browsers in the early hours. An inscription painted on a white wall is visible from afar: "Graineterie du Marché, specialist in garden supplies and seeds, pastas, rice, and dried legumes." The firm is the oldest seed shop in Paris and the decor of this cozy little boutique has not changed in fifty years. When the former owners bought the custom-designed green Formica fixtures at the Foire de Paris houseware show in 1958, they were at the cutting edge of contemporary style.

In 2004, José Ferré succumbed to the shop's retro charm and willingly left his former job to rescue the business, which was at risk of being converted into a convenience store. Customers come from far and wide to buy his specialties: all types of dried beans, including borlotti, haricots Tarbais (French white beans) for cassoulet, Soissons giant beans, and mogettes from the Vendée; black Beluga, green Puy, and Indian red lentils, as well as fava beans and chickpeas; buckwheat, as highly prized in Brittany as it is in Russia, where it is known as kasha; and rice of all kinds, from the Camargue or from Suriname. Most of the dried legumes and fruits, such as raisins, prunes, dates, and figs, are organic and sold loose by weight, as are the spices.

As for gardening supplies, packets of seeds are available in the back of the shop, which has been transformed into a delightful mini-flea market by José's wife. Outside, potted citronnella, fragrant herbs, vine stocks, and a few redcurrant and raspberry plants catch the eye of passing shoppers.

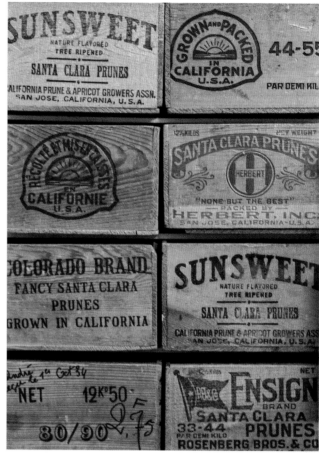

GRAINETERIE
DU MARCHÉ
Spécialiste en jardinage et graines

RÉF: 001

RÉF: 002

RÉF: 003

RÉF: 005

RÉF: 006

RÉF: 007

RÉF: 004

RÉF: 008

RÉF: 009

RÉF: 010

RÉF: 011

au 8, Place d'Aligre, Paris 12e

Traffic Jam

Fig. 2

762. PARIS — Le Marché de la Place d'Aligre   C. M.

Fig. 1

LIMONE SICIL.   AMORE

Mon secret...

LES GRAINES EN SACHETS
LE PAYSAN
en vente ici

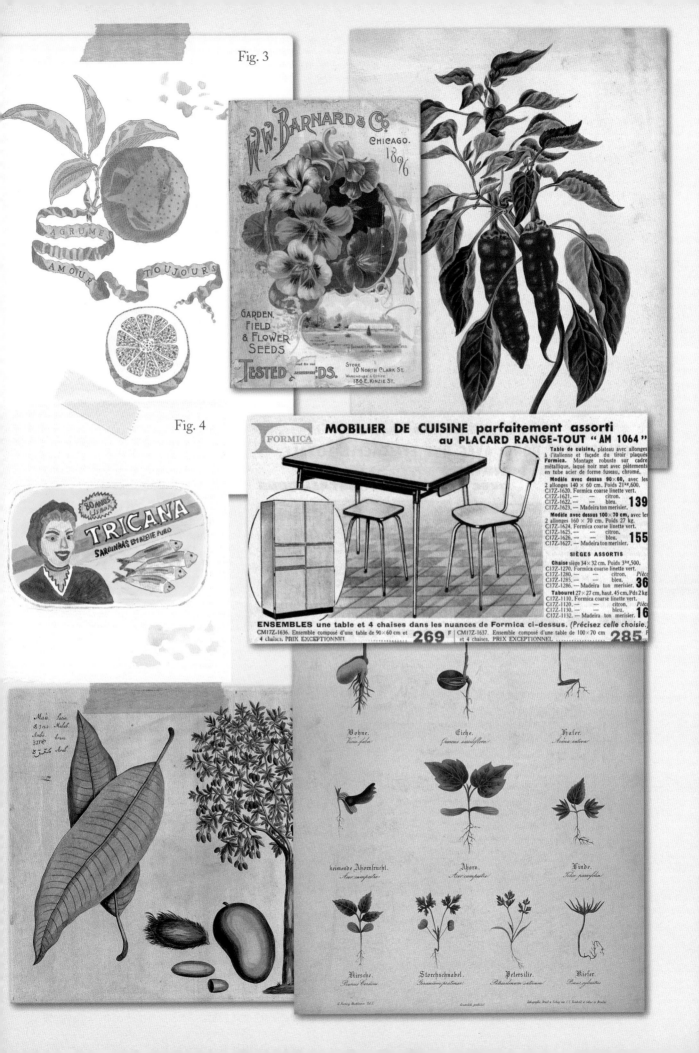

Fig. 3

AGRUMES
AMOUR TOUJOURS

W.W. BARNARD & Co.
CHICAGO.
1896

GARDEN,
FIELD
& FLOWER
SEEDS

TESTED SEEDS.

Store
10 NORTH CLARK ST.
WAREHOUSE & OFFICE
186 E. KINZIE ST.

Fig. 4

Bohne.
Vicia faba.

Eiche.
Quercus sessiliflora.

Hafer.
Avena sativa.

keimende Ahornfrucht.
Acer campestre.

Ahorn.
Acer campestre.

Linde.
Tilia parvifolia.

Hirsche.
Prunus Cerasus.

Storchschnabel.
Geranium pratense.

Petersilie.
Petroselinum sativum.

Kiefer.
Pinus sylvestris.

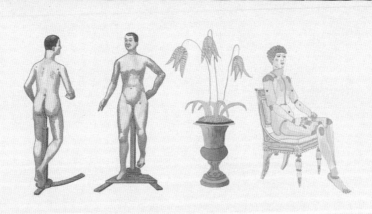

YVELINE ANTIQUES

4 RUE DE FURSTEMBERG — PARIS 6ᴱ

Since 1954, bargain hunters and curious passersby crossing
the enchanting Place Furstemberg have paused outside Yveline
Antiques—just next to Eugène Delacroix's former studio—
transfixed by its window displays populated with carefully
posed, strangely immobile figures. Articulated mannequins
of dark wood stand beside pale *capipotes*: wooden figures
of Madonnas and saints destined for religious processions,
which seem to bear the weight of years of faith and hope.
Agathe Derieux took over the store from her grandmother,
Yveline Lecerf, in 2013. As a child, she spent hours here
on a Saturday, by her grandmother's side, in rooms
that evoked a fairy-tale castle: crystal chandeliers,
baroque candelabra, countless antique silvered mirrors,
and portraits radiating gentleness and featuring gazes
that engage visitors in a silent dialogue.
Immersed in this atmosphere and guided by her grandmother,
Agathe learned all about the business over the years.
She shares Yveline's fascination with the human form:
"I love everything that evokes others, or portrays them."
Like Yveline, she has a particular fondness for painters'
mannequins. They resonate with memories of other times
and places that are mysterious and sometimes unsettling.
Introduced in the sixteenth century, these articulated
mannequins attained their peak popularity in the eighteenth
century, when they were painstakingly fashioned by master
artisans. Their wooden limbs are connected by an ingenious
internal system of hooks and strings, allowing them to be
posed in any position, from the fingertips to the toes.
Later, they were produced in series, but, even today,
these extraordinary figures collected by Agathe continue
to cast their spell.

GREEK SCULPTURE

Until the late nineteenth century,
Greek statues and busts were revered
by sculptors as representations of
the aesthetic ideal. From antiquity,
the Romans copied these works, and they
have served as archetypes of beauty
for artists through the ages.

ANTIQUITÉS ET CURIOSITÉS
YVELINE
ANTIQUES

RÉF: 001

RÉF: 002

RÉF: 003

RÉF: 004

RÉF: 005

RÉF: 006

RÉF: 007

RÉF: 007

RÉF: 008

RÉF: 009

4 RUE DE FURSTEMBERG, PARIS VIᴱ

Fig. 1

A. 408 ΔΕΛΦΟΙ. Ο ΑΝΤΙΝΟΟΣ. Ο ΕΥΝΟΟΥΜΕΝΟΣ ΤΟΥ ΑΔΡΙΑΝΟΥ - DELPHES. ANTINOUS. LE FAVORI DE L'EMPEREUR HADRIEN.
DELPHI. ANTINOUS. THE FAVOURITE OF THE EMPEROR HADRIAN - DELPHI. ANTINOOS. KAISER HADRIANS GUNSTLING.

The Insensible Perspiration

Published as the Act directs, June 20 1794. by E. Sibly.   Page sculp

HERCULES AND CORONA BOREALIS.

Fig. 2

♥

WITH THANKS TO

—

All of the owners of the boutiques,
ateliers, and museums featured here,
for the passion that drives them.
Ines for introducing me to Kate
and Julie, my invaluable editors
who follow me on each of my new
adventures!
Romain for his seasoned eye as the
best graphic designer in Paris.
My mom for the way she sees things.
My sister for her precious advice.
Alexis, the best teammate for
exploring such places.